ZAPATISTA
SPRING

Praise for *Zapatista Spring*:

"Ramor Ryan is a brilliant story-teller, and *Zapatista Spring* is impossible to put down. In this vivid account of democracy and solidarity in action, the pages overflow with humanity, wit, and the mountains and mud of Chiapas. This candid story should be read by anyone who has been inspired by the Zapatistas."

—*Ben Dangl, author of* Dancing with Dynamite

"*Zapatista Spring* doesn't read like a history book, and Ryan stops short of producing a personal memoir. Instead, it feels like cracking open an undated personal diary, which, thanks to the author's revolutionary sensibilities, storytelling skills, and sense of humor, translates into a hard-to-put-down read."

—*Dawn Paley, journalist and research associate with the North American Congress on Latin America*

"This book is a much-needed counterforce—sympathetic but relentless—to the formulaic proclamations of armchair Zapatistas everywhere. Weaving between story and theory, cynicism and mutual aid, development and despair, Ryan offers an insider's view of the heart of shades at the core of the Zapatista solidarity movement."

—*Richard J.F. Day, author of* Gramsci Is Dead

"Are you ready to join the motherfuckin' resistance? Well, this job is not for the squeamish or pampered, it's tough fuckin' work. Ramor Ryan doesn't just speak theoretically about the Zapatistas, he lived and worked amongst them. This firsthand account of the most inspiring resistance movement of the turn of the century is a must read for anyone wanting to learn how the Zapatistas did it."

—*Franklin López, Producer of subMedia.TV*

ZAPATISTA SPRING

Anatomy of a Rebel Water Project

& The Lessons of International Solidarity

RAMOR RYAN

AK PRESS
EDINBURGH · OAKLAND · BALTIMORE

Zapatista Spring: Anatomy of a Rebel Water Project
& The Lessons of International Solidarity
© 2011 Ramor Ryan

This edition © 2011 AK Press (Oakland, Edinburgh, Baltimore)
ISBN : 978-1-84935-072-3 | eBook ISBN: 978-1-84935-073-0
Library of Congress Control Number: 2011925323

AK Press   AK Press
674-A 23rd Street   PO Box 12766
Oakland, CA 94612   Edinburgh, EH8 9YE
USA   Scotland
www.akpress.org   www.akuk.com
akpress@akpress.org   ak@akedin.demon.co.uk

The above addresses would be delighted to provide you with the latest AK Press distribution catalog, which features the several thousand books, pamphlets, zines, audio and video products, and stylish apparel published and/or distributed by AK Press. Alternatively, visit our websites for the complete catalog, latest news, and secure ordering.

Visit us at:
www.akpress.org | www.akuk.com | www.revolutionbythebook.akpress.org.

Printed in Canada on acid-free, recycled paper with union labor.
Cover and interior artwork by Tim Simons (timsimonsgraphics.net).
All Photos by Francesc Parés. Photographs were taken with the full permission of the community and project workers.

While this book is based on true events, some characters and scenes have been fictionalized.

Ramor Ryan would like to thank: The Institute for Anarchist Studies for early financial support; Tauno, Jim, and Michael for critique and ideas; and Zach and Lorna at AK Press for doing a great job in publishing the book. Finally, *mil gracias* to the Zapatista base communities for receiving us and the *compañeros* and *compañeras* of the solidarity water teams for sharing these magnificent times.

—for Ixim

So that you will know a little of from where you came.

Contents

Prelude.

Bridge across the Jungle

Deep in the Lacandon Jungle, we walk with the *compañeros*[1] and come upon a giant tree. The lone Ceiba reaches sublimely over the immense matted forest canopy, sun sparkling amongst the dense matrix of its dispersing limbs. The massive buttress around the base lends the trees a spectacular, even stellar diameter.

We stop in our tracks and gaze in awe at one of the last remnants of a once-great towering forest of tropical trees, some over sixty meters high.

This beautiful, forlorn survivor, I muse.

"Magnificent, no?"

The compañero Zapatista by my side nods in agreement.

"It would make a fine canoe, compa," he says to the companion by his side.

The other *campesino*[2] takes a swipe at the ground-level vines with his machete.

"A fine canoe that would take us all the way up north!"

He turns to his companion and they wistfully discuss chopping down the tree in order to fashion the mother of all canoes.

"You can't chop down the tree!" I say, appalled.

"No, of course not," says the compañero Zapatista.

"It's a sacred tree. It is forbidden to cut it down," he says with a distinct sense of disappointment.

We walk on through the jungle path in silence. Praxedis, the other outsider of our party, senses my bewilderment.

"What's wrong?" he asks.

"I like trees. Especially grand old Ceibas."

---

1. I promise to keep the number of Spanish words to a minimum, but *compañero*, a more intimate form of comrade, is an indispensable word.
2. *Campesino*: a subsistence farmer, or peasant.

"Yeah I hear you. It is a nice tree," he says, "but think of it from the peasants' perspective. They don't see Mother Earth as some romantic thing to look at. They see it as the sustenance of their families, as the means to live."

I know, I know.

As a solidarity activist inserting myself into the culture of the indigenous compañeros, I should be paying more attention to de-colonizing myself of my internal oppressions.

"Let every grand Ceiba fall before a campesino be refrained from reaching the north in a canoe!" I declare facetiously, most definitely externalizing my oppressions and setting my process of de-colonization back several decades.

But, in reality, I'm not sure that I am manifesting paternalistic or arrogant posturing in the instance of this tree—or not the tree, but the environment. It is about something else, about different ways of seeing things...

It's how I look upon the lone tree and see a dying planet, wracked by capitalist destruction (here in the forest: the lumber trade), and yet the compañero Zapatista looks upon the same object and sees a means to go somewhere. Or a sacred object connecting the terrestrial world with the spirit world above. Of course, what one sees is relative to one's position in time and space, and here specifically there are cultural and economic factors underpinned by privilege and poverty.

This vignette serves only as a perfunctory caveat—nothing is ever as it seems, and people gaze upon the same object with admiration but often for distinctly different reasons.

And here is the dilemma as we engage in the earnest revolutionary activity of building a new world together. If solidarity is unity of purpose or togetherness, how to span this great divide of inequality, privilege, universal rights, political agency, and even our seeing things completely differently?

In constructing this great bridge of international solidarity across the globe, where do we even begin?

I.

Journey into the Desert of Solitude

"I am here and support the Zapatistas because in a world full of lies, I believe and trust them."—Eduardo Galeano

The Theater of Action

Roberto Arenas is a small Tzeltal[1] community of twenty-three subsistence farmer families located in the Chiapas Lacandon Rainforest, a six-hour drive from the nearest major commercial center, the market town of Ocosingo. The occupants, adherents of the Zapatista National Liberation Army (EZLN, its Spanish acronym), formed a *nuevo poblado*, a new community, here about three years ago. The land makes up part of the territory that was taken over or "recuperated" by the Zapatistas in the midst of the January 1st 1994 uprising, as the land owners fled and the rebels took control of the zone. Under the mantle that the land is owned by those who work it, the Zapatistas began slowly dividing out the vast swathes to Zapatista militia and support base families—usually landless indigenous peasants or campesinos who previously labored on large *fincas* under difficult conditions. About 300,000 hectares of land were recuperated by the insurgent Zapatistas after the tumultuous state-wide uprising. The newly formed community of Roberto Arenas fell under the jurisdiction of the Francisco Gomez Autonomous region, a self-governing Zapatista municipality where there is no state authority and, as the sign entering the municipality announces, "Here the people govern and the government obeys!"

Like hundreds of other little villages dotted throughout the region, theirs is a community characterized by pastoral simplicity. The roughly hewn, earthen floor dwellings are scattered around the undulating hills and converge on a grassy community plaza with a muddy basketball court, flanked by a couple of rustic wooden

---

1. The Tzeltal are an ethnic indigenous group of the Maya family numbering some 400,000 located mainly in the east-central of Chiapas. The language spoken by the people is also called Tzeltal.

structures that serve as church, community hall, and school. Although the community would probably be considered to exist in extreme poverty by any standard indices, they are poor mostly in the sense that they lack buying power—surviving on less than $2 a day. Nevertheless, all vital needs of daily life are satisfied with farming and the natural resources around them, and only a small part of their needs are satisfied in the market. Roberto Arenas is a frugal rather than impoverished community, it is self-sufficient in a traditional way, and would only approach extreme poverty if they lost the forests, rivers, and commons that are part of their home.

Like most other indigenous settlements in the region, Roberto Arenas has no electricity or potable water. Water for washing is hauled from the jungle river and drinking water is carried from a small water-hole 1 kilometer away. There are few latrines, and, as is customary, adults and children alike mostly use the natural surroundings. Almost all water sources are contaminated by human and animal feces. Waterborne illnesses affect the population (predominantly children) including those related to amoebas and giardia, and there is a threat of cholera and typhoid. Lack of potable water sources increase the risk of scabies infection, lice, salmonella, ascariasis and enterovirus diarrheas.

Good, sweet water is available from an abundant freshwater spring 2 km up the mountain, but is unattainable as the villagers lack everything they need to pipe it into the community. The cost of basic materials like pipes and tools is beyond the community budget, and they lack the technical know-how to implement such a project. Historically, generations of colonizers of the Lacandon Jungle dealt with this problem by taking basic precautions like adding iodine or boiling the water—but these are inadequate. Some communities would make do with the most basic of water systems, budget allowing—a makeshift concoction of pipes connected to the nearest water source. If the community was fortunate it might get some institutional support from non-governmental organizations (NGOs), charities, or church organizations. In a region where the government does nothing to provide basic services, water systems are few and far between. The lack of this basic necessity, added to the long list of communities' grievances and the injustices suffered, ultimately resulted in the Zapatista uprising. Off the political map in the eyes of the state, they are ignored and cast into the void. So, typical for the region, Roberto Arenas has received no institutional support from either government or NGOs.

Without government or state, how does political autonomy work in the Zapatista zone? How do the people organize to get things done, like realizing a water system for the community? In Roberto Arenas, like all Zapatista villages, the community assembly—with representatives from each household—meets in the community hall, weekly—or more frequently if there are things to decide. Together they determine the manner and method of developing their own village, taking into account what resources are available. Decisions are made by the assembly, preferably by consensus. If there is a split and no clear decision, the debates and discussions go on until the assembly reaches a consensus. Occasionally, this can take days on end. This is participatory democracy in action, warts and all.

This kind of assembly-based decision-making process is not unique to the Zapatistas: indigenous communities throughout the region have always worked like this, most likely since pre-colonial times. It is in this forum, that all the major decisions concerning the community are taken—from land issues to community development, to justice—and are then passed on to the relevant commission for fine tuning. The decision to join the Zapatistas and go to war on January 1st, 1994 was taken in such an assembly. And if asked what influence the EZLN has had on the traditional community assembly procedures, compañeros and compañeras will mention how more women and youth are now involved in the decision making than before. Previously the assemblies were dominated by older male members but with Zapatista influence, the old patriarchal ties are not as binding.

So it was that Roberto Arenas decided that their biggest priority was getting a fresh water supply. This necessity was prioritized over other pressing needs, like electricity, new work tools, a hammock bridge to span the river that separated them from the dirt road, and the construction of a church building.

The assembly nominated three water "commissioners" to investigate the matter and to petition the local autonomous council for help and support. The three made their preliminary survey of what would be needed and walked the arduous mountain paths through the jungle, arriving at La Garrucha, the regional autonomous

municipality center. They attended the weekly council meetings—
or juntas—overseen by the council representatives there by rotation,
and attended by community members from any of the several hundred communities in this particular autonomous municipality (one
of seven throughout the Zapatista zone of influence). This system of
local governance is part of their aspiration to organize in a participatory manner, from the bottom-up instead of the top-down. The
Zapatista slogan—to lead by obeying—captures this concept.

The de facto autonomy of the Zapatista zone is a result of the
never-ratified San Andres Accords on Indigenous Rights and Culture negotiated between the EZLN and the Mexican government
in 1996. Under provisions of the agreement approved but never
sanctioned by the government, majority indigenous municipalities
would be granted limited autonomy over land, habitat, exploitation of natural resources, the environment, education, health, and
agrarian policies. Authorities and municipal posts would be designated by traditional *usos y costumbres*[2] instead of being divided up

---

2. Uses and customs. A phrase meaning the traditions of the indigenous
communities.

among political parties. In response to the government's betrayal of the San Andres agreements, the Zapatistas set up autonomous structures without official state authorization. Such pirate action has resulted in a burgeoning and successful system of rebel autonomy that exists under the constant threat of dismantlement by the Mexican Army.

The three *compas* of Roberto Arenas patiently wait their turn at the autonomous municipality seat of La Garrucha, prosaically entitled the Good Government Council "The Path of the Future" Caracol. The wait could be days as the business of the municipal council is long and complicated, but eventually they will present their petition. The various representatives listen, take note of the petition, and discuss the project. Everything is taken into account and the three compas return to their village to await the outcome.

The good government committee of the autonomous municipality refer the case to their elected water commission and the options are weighed. The commission consults various parties including the local EZLN commander and clandestine committee members, and so, in the end, after the issue has been bandied around what seems like half the inhabitants of this particular region of the jungle, the community of Roberto Arenas is notified about the eligibility of their request. It's a process similar to what happens anywhere in the world at a local council level, except for one significant difference: the state authorities have no involvement whatsoever; this is an autonomous process overseen by the communities' people. There is no separation between who is governed and who is governing—they are one and the same. The various committees and bodies are overseen not by elected or appointed officials, but by members of the community, a duty performed by rotation. Here, in a place off the map, a nowhere of sorts, the people have adopted an enlightened form of governance. This is how an autonomous administration functions. This is peoples' power in action.

And, most significantly, for this particular little story, the decision for the community is... Affirmative! Yes to assigning a water project to Roberto Arenas! So the momentum to bring potable water to the isolated rural community on recuperated Zapatista lands begins. Now to find a way to make it happen!

Not surprisingly, the Zapatista autonomous municipalities are chronically lacking in funding and resources. Revenue comes from their own base—from Zapatista agricultural ventures like coffee or honey, from NGOs (local, national, and international) and from solidarity groups. In the case of getting water to a base community, the municipalities have a couple of options: A fairly basic project—a DIY job—can be self-financed, though is often only a temporary solution. A more sophisticated water system is very costly and requires that local engineers and plumbers be hired to oversee the project. Another option is to petition an NGO or solidarity group to support and realize a community water project.

Enter the Water Boys and Girls of Solidarity

The first solidarity-inspired water projects in Zapatista-liberated territory occurred about six months after the 1994 uprising and the initial consolidation of a rebel zone. Activists who had been embedded in Central American war zones during the 1980s arrived to employ their skills, seeing what was happening as a continuation of the anti-imperialist struggle in places like El Salvador, Nicaragua, and Guatemala. The first water projects were initiated in strategically important communities—like Patiwitz, historical kernel of Zapatista insurgence that was now suffering an internal division because of a split between the main families. The water project had the potential to re-unite the community around a single vital initiative, a piped water system supplying all shared community places—school, church, village basketball court, collective kitchen, etc. Even with the first small projects, the political capital involved in water systems became obvious. A water project not only supplied a village with potable water, but represented a potent political weapon, as well.

More Zapatista sympathizers arrived from other places—around the country and world—keen to get involved in a hands-on way in the Chiapas struggle. One could spend days or weeks idling around a rustic peace camp, accompanying the rebels, or participating in more office-based work like media, fundraising, or compiling human rights reports in San Cristobal de las Casas (the picturesque colonial town that is the region's administrative center and tourist hang out). But volunteering on water projects seemed the most practical way to get stuck in, to get your hands dirty (and blistered), and start digging, mixing cement, laying pipes, assembling tap-stands, shoulder to shoulder with the compañeros, the indigenous men, women, and children in the remote and isolated jungle or mountainous communities.

Water projects were a favored occupation in solidarity work, particularly among the more direct-action-oriented, anarcho crowd. By the end of 1996, the initial wave of water project development workers with roots in NGOs, church and Central American leftist organizations gave way to a fresh new generation of activists who were generally more inspired by the Zapatista model and had a history of anti-authoritarian, anti-systemic organizing in their homelands. So it was that the Water Project collectives came together and formed self-organized and autonomous groups that oversaw the construction of fairly basic, but quite efficient, gravity-fed clean water systems for Zapatista-affiliated communities. Crucially, in turning the NGO-recipient relationship upside down, the solidarity workers operated under the broad jurisdiction of the Zapatista autonomous councils. It was the indigenous peasant campesinos themselves, through their own organization, who decided where and how the national and international solidarity workers went. In a sense, the water project collectives served the Zapatistas. The initial question—what can we do to help the Zapatistas?—tempered by the fire of experience, with a salsa picante of ideology became: What is it that the Zapatistas want us to do?

The point of intersection, or *encuentro*, between the Zapatista insurgents/base of support and outsiders is in the designated centers in five locations around the rebel zone. Originally known as *aguascalientes* (after the famous point of meeting of the revolutionary armies of Pancho Villa and Emiliano Zapata outside Mexico City during the Mexican Revolution), they later became known as the *caracoles* (snails, representing slow, solid progress forward)—a place for political and movement connectivity. And it is here, in these important physical spaces, that indigenous base and solidarity activists join, face-to-face, not as idealized figures, but as human beings in the flesh.

So it was that the three Tzeltal compañeros from the isolated hamlet of Roberto Arenas (population 200) came down from the mountains to speak to the autonomous council of the La Garrucha caracol (population 300) and present their petition for a water system. So it also was that three compañeros from the water project collective came into the jungle from their base in the old colonial town of San Cristobal (population 100,000) in the central highlands of Chiapas, to talk with the autonomous council about their next project...

In what must be considered an extraordinary and fine thing in this day and age of homogeneity, two distinct and unequal worlds merge, indigenous and solidarity workers, find common ground, and begin to work together. And underlining the radical or even revolutionary nature of the endeavor, they attempt to go beyond solidarity—with all its somewhat paternalistic interpretations—and towards reciprocity. People helping each other in the spirit of mutual aid.

Journey into the Desert of Solitude

What must Don Sisifo and his two water commission delegates from Roberto Arenas have thought when they set eyes on us—the three "water technicians," Maria, Praxedis and me—for the first time that morning in La Garrucha?

In our defense, we were weary and disheveled, having left San Cristobal at 2 AM to avoid military and migration checkpoints on the five-hour drive into the rebel zone. We had a pickup truck full of work equipment and our two foreigners violated tourist visas by entering the designated "conflict zone." The federal army checkpoint approaching La Garrucha had, surprisingly, been manned as early as 5 AM. We knew their routine by now, and it was very unusual that the troops were out so early.

"Fuck," says Maria.

We slow down as we approach. The young soldier is taking his time to come out.

"You know what? Fuck this," says Maria.

In a decisive act of insolence, she speeds up, swings the 4 Wheel Drive to the other side of the dirt road and drives past the checkpoint. She waves prettily at the guard, who is standing there somewhat dumbfounded, his rifle still by his side.

And we are gone. Around the bend and into the darkness.

"Maria!"

"Fuck them, we've got more important things to do than be detained by those assholes."

"You have no respect for armed men, Maria," laughs Praxedis.

I remember meeting Maria for the first time a couple of years ago and thinking she came across as quite straight, quite conventional, with the competitive air of a typically ambitious NGO operative. It was a delight to see the mischievous, subversive, and positively scandalous side of her emerge as she engaged more with the Zapatista milieu and copper fastened her political outlook to the extent that she was now one of the most staunch and diehard Zapatista activists around. She still looks totally straight and her militancy is veiled behind a hard-working, hyper-organized, and very capable public persona. Running the military road-block at dawn is definitely a courageous, through somewhat reckless act, but such is Maria: determined and ready to take a chance or two.

So we pull into the nearby Zapatista caracol and feel safe, enveloped in its bosom. The soldiers won't or can't pursue us in here.

The Roberto Arenas delegation receives us and we are tired and weary, scruffily attired and resembling a punk rock trio with a penchant for survivalist expeditions. The three campesinos look like...well, three campesinos. Dark rugged faces burnt from the sun; strong, short, angular bodies clad in well-worn, much scrubbed and somewhat ragamuffin clothes. Each carries a machete.

Introductions are modestly made and hands are shaken. Don Sisifo,[3] the community leader does the talking while Juan, his teenage son, busies himself with saddling the horses. Completing their

---

3. Don is like a polite form of "Mr." It denotes a certain authority and bequests respect.

party is Alfredo,[4] a brawny young man who, Don Sisifo informs us, has been designated one of the water *responsables* (in charge of, responsible for the water project) and will work closely with us. Alfredo carries himself with some pride. This is apparently the first major post (*cargo*) of responsibility given to him by the community and he is keen and attentive. We introduce ourselves—Praxedis[5] from Mexico City, Maria from the USA, and me, from Ireland.

"Are you from a foreign NGO?" asks Sisifo.

"No," explains Maria, "we don't work for any state institution or formal NGO, we are autonomous solidarity workers. That means we are not sent here by anybody, but come here as activists in solidarity with the Zapatista struggle. We are here to work together doing water projects, not just to bring the community sweet water, but also to strengthen rebel autonomy against the *malgobierno* [the unjust government]."

The campesinos thank us for our solidarity with the cause and for helping the community. Don Sisifo addresses us as "compañeros" and "compañera" which is a noteworthy first step. They seem extremely shy and reticent and we think it might be that they are not terribly confident communicating in Spanish. Unfortunately, none of us speaks their mother tongue, Tzeltal.

Since the autonomous municipality authorities granted us permission to conduct an initial feasibility study, we propose that we get to work immediately, to draw up an engineering and work plan with the community, and sign a contract. If all goes well, within about eight to ten weeks, there should be a functioning system delivering clean water into the homes of the village occupants. The campesinos nod readily in agreement.

"*Esta bien*—it's all good," says Don Sisifo, hurriedly. "*Vámonos.*" Let's go.

He doesn't mean to be impolite, but points out that we have a long trek ahead of us and it is best to get going right away, to avoid having to cross the mountain under the scorching midday sun. Don Sisifo tells us we have a five and a half hour hike ahead of us. Three horses carry the water system equipment and materials

---

4. All names of Zapatistas have been changed to protect the identity of the individuals.
5. All names and identities of water technicians have been changed as a measure of protection.

and we three carry our own backpacks. Sisifo and his teenage son lead the horses, and we plod along in the mud after them while Alfredo takes up the rear.

Before us looms a horizon of mountains and forest. It may not be the heart of darkness, but the Lacandon Jungle has its specters, and is known colloquially as the Desert of Solitude. Once, this vast, lush rainforest, covering 6,000 square kilometers[6] was mostly un-inhabited, but waves of twentieth-century migration by disposed and landless migrants from Oaxaca and Guerrero ensured the slow but steady colonization of this virgin territory. By the 1980s, the rainforest was reduced to about one-third of its original size as, alongside the massive colonization, the government intensified exploitation of the forest with logging and mineral extraction, and large-scale cattle ranching cut vast swathes of pasture from forestland. In this fertile wilderness, campesinos cut out a basic living. The population increased from a few thousand to roughly 400,000. Industry and subsistence farming came in conflict over limited resources. The migrants were caught between their own farming and seasonal work as peons on the farm estates or coffee plantations of wealthy landowners. Poverty and misery, pervaded by a sense of hopelessness, was their lot. Despite the promise offered by the forests, canyons, and glens of the Lacandon region, from the back lands of Chiapas came not development or progress but its antithesis: rebellion. Some people's solitude or fear is other people's refuge. It was here amongst the population—the poorest of the poor—that the Zapatista resistance took root. As Sub-comandante Marcos has remarked, "That's why the Lacandon is what it is—a kind of breathing space at the end of the country." For ten years the Zapatista rebellion grew in the shadows of the Lacandon Jungle and emerged on January 12th, 1994, as a state-wide insurgency. And so, from a semantic perspective, from the Desert of Solitude was born the War against Oblivion.

The sun is already climbing in the sky and making its presence known as we set off on the trail. With a coordination that no doubt impresses our hosts, I manage to slip and tumble into the river as we cross a rickety bridge. Don Sisifo helps me out of the knee-deep

---

6. Originally the Lacandon Rainforest covered an area of about 19,000 square kilometers. This is about the size of the Basque Country or Chechnya. A half century of colonization and industry reduced the forest area by two-thirds.

water (politely not laughing, while Maria and Praxedis laugh heartily in unison), and I silently curse myself and my shitty Doc Marten boots, which are already falling apart, and now are drenched to boot. Every step becomes painful.

The first part of the trek is through green, fertile land, and the trail is covered in deep mud—sometimes up to our knees. Around us, as far as the eye can see, are cultivated fields, corn plots, and some cattle pasture. Soon we emerge from this lush ecosystem and begin the climb up the steep paths of the mountainside into more arid territory. After a couple of grueling hours hiking up rough trails, we come upon a bleak ridge, free of agriculture, barren except for a smattering of rugged trees and sparse bush. We sit and take a rest, thirstily sipping at our water supplies. The sun is rising high in the sky and the heat is becoming unbearable.

We use the moment's respite to ask a few questions of the compas. It's like extracting blood from a stone, but we do manage to get them talking a little.

"My family came to this region in the 1970s," Don Sisifo tells us. "We left Oxchuc in the Highlands because there was no more land there. My father joined a group coming to occupy land in the canyons. But the land was poor and we had to keep moving deeper into the mountains. And when the Zapatistas came to the region, many campesinos joined the organization and plans were made for a big land takeover.

"How many campesinos joined the organization in this region?" I ask.

"I don't know. A lot. Thousands!"

"What happened then?"

"After the uprising in '94, the owners fled and the compañeros took all this land, and so it became re-occupied land. The organization divided the land up between the communities and here we remain."

How about in Roberto Arenas? Is the land good there?

"Yes, the land is very good. We are the first to plant there. The land gives a lot."

"And how many Zapatista communities are there in the region?"

"Well, I think about fifty. Some have left the organization."

"Why?"

"*Saber*," he says with a shrug. Who knows...

Now he seems a little uneasy with the interrogation. It is clear that Don Sisifo is a man of few words and he gets a bit flustered. It's like he doesn't like hanging around indulging in idle banter.

"Let's go. We have a long way yet."

The sun beats down, the mountain trail gets steeper and we are all sweating profusely. Another hour's hike up the mountain trail and I'm really feeling it. As I trudge on through the muddy trail, heavily, wearily, all I can do is watch my step on the slippery surface and feel the pain of my bedraggled boots—my wet, squelching boots—and wince with each step as my backpack digs into my back, rubbing raw against my aching shoulder-blades. This backpack is just too heavy and I feel like ditching my beloved books— Conrad's colonial atrocity, *Heart of Darkness*; one of B. Traven's Chiapas novels, *The Rebellion of the Hanged*; and Albert Camus's *The Myth of Sisyphus*. I can actually imagine feeling the weight of those small volumes pressing against my back. But no, I can't ditch them. Reading by candlelight in the depth of night in the jungle communities is my greatest joy. Fucking intellectual. I'd more quickly dump the heavy metal water valves I'm carrying in a bat of an eye. But I can't; the whole water system won't work without them. So I'm not sure if it is the pain of my swollen, lacerated feet in my shitty boots, or the ton weight of my backpack rubbing my shoulders and back raw that hurts most. Or maybe the aching thirst, since our water supplies were depleted long ago. It seems the two liters of water per person we packed is not even half enough for an arduous trek like this. I stumble along, somewhat delirious, and concentrate on just getting through the march, laboriously placing one heavy foot in front of the other. The compas, noticing my troubles, offer to take my pack but I refuse, my pride offended.

But finally, about five hours in, the climbing part is mostly over, and after a final push upwards, we reach the crest and are soon heading slowly downwards into the valley. We descend into the verdant green basin of the Jataté River and here the moist, tropical terrain is cultivated with corn fields and plantain and coffee plantations. Almost at the end of our tether, it's a huge relief to, at last, arrive at river's edge, to feel its cool beautiful jungle freshness and fill our empty water bottles. But we must wait an excruciating twenty minutes of parched pain for the iodine to sanitize the water. I don't have the will to wait and take a chance after ten minutes, wolfing down the most delightful liquid I have ever tasted in my life. I am perfectly aware that I will no doubt pay for this impatient indulgence in the days ahead with the runs and cramps, but I don't care; I am dehydrated and feel like I'm literally dying of thirst. The campesinos eye us with amusement. I notice they don't appear to even be breaking much of a sweat. As we sprawl about under the shade of an old tree, gulping down water after our heroic march, the campesinos tell us that they set out before dawn to meet us in Garrucha, climbing this very mountain—and so this was their second trip today. Even though Maria, Praxedis, and I have worked in these mountains for a good while now, and are in excellent shape, we feel pretty useless at this very moment.

Enjoying a second wind, we stroll the last stretch and finally, five and half hours after we set out, the forest parts and we enter into the flat plain of the village. Roberto Arenas is a picturesque settlement nestled by the side of the broad, majestic Jataté River, surrounded by lush, fertile—if hilly—land. The community center is located on a wide grassy knoll, flanked on one side by a wooden shack serving as a school, and another that serves as a church.

Beyond the village center, there is a scattering of rough, dirt-floored huts where the people live. Despite the rural frugality, it is a very calm and beautiful place. It is not like the other Zapatista villages where I've been. There is a strange quietude, an absence of children, and the lack of colourful murals is apparent, unusual for a Zapatista community. Don Sisifo leads us to the school building and apologizes for our rough quarters. No, we all say, it's wonderful. But where is everyone?

"They are shy. Visitors are unusual here. But you will meet the people soon."

I notice a few colorfully dressed women peek out shyly from the darkened doorways, and little by little, bands of ragged, shoeless children come out to stare at us, too timid to approach or engage us.

We wave at them and they dart back into the shadows of their houses.

Beneath the tin roof, on few sparse boards serving as walls, we three hang our hammocks and finally rest.

Some time later the good Don Sisifo brings us to his kitchen, and his wife Dolores serves us beans and tortillas, as numerous little kids run around the place. After the long hike, it feels like one of the finest meals of our lives and we eat with such savage appetite that the children laugh at us. Doña Dolores shoos them away. She is a quiet, industrious, middle-aged woman, who speaks to us in a mix of Tzeltal and Spanish, smiles a lot, and makes us feel welcome. Don Sisifo, who is starting to relax a bit more with us and overcome his shyness, begins to explain the situation in the community, the lack of everything—running water, electricity, latrines, a health clinic, teachers for the school, transport to the nearest town, even the lack of basic farming tools. These people have nothing, absolutely nothing except their land, their will to work, and their pride in being Zapatistas. Sisifo himself, he tells us, has been a Zapatista for sixteen years.

How must things have been before he was a Zapatista or before he farmed this occupied land?

Before he has a chance to answer, Alfredo, the water *responsable* comes in and whispers in his ear.

"It is time," announces Don Sisifo. "The compañeros from the water commission have assembled and are ready to receive you. Let's go."

We thank Doña Dolores for the food with such overt gratitude that she must think we are a bit mad. She just stands there
shaking her head and smiling widely.

"We are happy that you have come," she says, a gaggle of children hanging from her apron and skirts.

Our first working meeting takes place in the rustic, bare
schoolroom, sitting somewhat squashed at a child-sized wooden
bench and tables, initially with just the two members of the
water commission—Alfredo and Vicente—and Don Sisifo. They
describe the different options for fresh water supplies, the location
of various springs in the surrounding hills and their attributes. We
decide the most likely option is a spring some 2 km from the community, situated high enough in the hills to deal with the problem
of head or gravity for the water to flow with enough power. The
compañeros had begun trying to construct their own water system here last year, DIY style, but ran short on funds. Maria has
the most technical and on-the-ground experience of our team and
takes charge of the questions and answers.

"Considering this option," she says, "it sounds like it should be a pretty straight-forward system. But we need to do the survey to be absolutely certain."

Little by little, as dusk falls, more men and children, returning from their day's work in the *milpa*[7] drift in and gather around our meeting table until there is meeting quorum. In the near pitch darkness of the schoolroom, the men of the community gather around a couple of candles. There is something archaic and holy about the atmosphere, the quiet murmuring, the shadows moving about, the shy humble campesinos, all wearing ragged shirts and pants and boots, shaking our hands and thanking us for coming.

Eventually, all the men and youths of the community are present, as well as a gaggle of pre-teen boys and girls. No women are present because, as we are told, they are preparing the evening meal in their kitchens. Despite the use of water being one of the main preserves of the women—bathing kids, cooking, washing—water systems are perceived as men's work in the traditional, conservative culture of indigenous communities such as this one.

It is the women (and children) who benefit most directly from piped water in the communities, since it is they who have to bear the burden of carrying the water on their shoulders from the stream or nearest well to the kitchen every single day. On average, they spend about an hour a day fetching water, carrying the ten or fifteen liter vessel *mecopal*[8] style, with a strap supported by their forehead. Some women balance whole jugs of water on their heads. It is grueling work, balancing this weight on your head over hills and along muddy tracks to the house.

"We will need some women representatives on the water committee," says Maria.

"Yes," says Don Sisifo, "we will talk to them."

Maria takes the lead as our primary spokesperson. At first the campesinos seem confused, looking to me and Praxedis to lead. But as they see us deferring to Maria, they soon enough accept her authority. She speaks slowly and clearly for the benefit of those with basic Spanish, and allows time for a little translation into Tzeltal

---

7. A *milpa* is a corn field plot, where the campesino grows the three basics: corn, beans, and pumpkin.
8. *Mecopal* is a traditional way of carrying sacks or jugs on one's back with a rope wrapped around the forehead.

to be done. She explains how we are going to use the most basic, gravity-fed system to pipe water into each house in the community, that the process will take about two or maybe three months depending on the pace of work, and if all goes to plan, the system will function for at least twenty years—more if it is maintained well. The system will consist of 2 km of plastic PVC piping running from the spring to a 13,000 liter cement reservoir tank situated in the village. This will allow for a perennial water supply for every family in the village and take into account a 3.5% annual population growth.

Ultimately, the idea is to not just install the water system, but to train the people at the same time, so they can manage their own system, and maintain and repair it as the years pass. They themselves will oversee the system and all its workings. I reflect: how many people in my world know how their own plumbing system works, beyond turning on the tap? Here these people will learn it all, from source to tap, and this will become part of the arsenal of their community autonomy.

Maria outlines what each party's responsibilities are. We will all work side by side, but everyone has their more specific role: those in the water team will concentrate on the technical stuff, while community members will provide the labor and a willingness to learn. We solidarity workers will share the burden of the back-breaking work, but our skills lie in the technical field, and Maria emphasizes, we are not bosses, nor well-paid NGO agents; we are fellow compas, and down with the Zapatista struggle.

A compañero called Gordo—i.e. Fatso, because he is slightly less lean than the rest of his fellow campesinos—who is the sometime school teacher and best Spanish speaker in the community, steps forward.

"Who pays you to be here then?" asks Gordo. A fair question.

"No one pays us, but we get stipends from the water group to cover our expenses. The water group raises money from people who support the work we do. People give money as their form of solidarity with the Zapatista struggle."

The compañeros discuss this information at length and quite animatedly.

Gordo turns to us after a while and, summing up their conversation with some brevity, says, "But, the compas want to know why you are here if nobody sent you and nobody is paying you."

We three visitors look at each other. Christ. International Solidarity—where to begin? Do we start with the international brigades supporting the anti-fascist struggle in republican Spain, 1936? We could begin with what it is not: we are not development workers. It is not about charity. We are not here to provide a safety net for the absence of government infrastructure.

Praxedis, generally a quiet, taciturn person, steps up to explain, putting forward a political and somewhat philosophical explanation:

"It is about political and social justice, compañeros. What can we do to move the Zapatista struggle and the process of autonomy forward? We do it by working together, side by side, with unity of purpose. While we construct the water system together, we will share our basic engineering knowledge with you, and you will be teaching us the ways of the indigenous Zapatista communities. And learning together we not only build a water system, but we also build a bridge of solidarity between both of our political communities, bringing them closer. This is how constructing a water system becomes a concrete manifestation of our solidarity with your rebel autonomy."

Maria and I stare at him, impressed and feel like bursting out into spontaneous applause. Right on, Praxedis.

After conferring with the compañeros, Gordo turns to address us.

"The compas say they are glad that you are here and support the struggle. They offer to build a kitchen for you, and they will bring tortillas and firewood for your duration here—to help with your expenses."

We offer our thanks in return. We are off to a good start. However it's getting late and we are ready to sleep. Maria wraps up the meeting, thanking everyone for receiving us. A few questions are asked and then everyone there signs a contract. Many of the men are completely illiterate and sign with a symbol.

The long meeting winds down and the compañeros approach us one-by-one, shyly shaking our hands and thanking us for coming. It is quite moving, and despite being exhausted, the gesture gives us a little more energy and raises our spirit. We chat a while, answering questions about how many hours it took to travel from our home cities and such like, and finally the last of the compas departs. We three exhausted solidarity activists, a long way from home, hitch our hammocks and fall into deep slumber, despite the swarms of mosquitoes and chaquistas[9] biting us. Each bite is a sting, each sting inducing a feverish effect. Sleep comes as a mighty relief.

The Cartography of Thirst

I awake but feel as if I haven't slept. It rained heavily during the night, and the open-sided schoolroom allowed all the valley's bugs to take shelter under our laminated roof. My face is covered in chaquista bites, and feels aflame. The mosquitoes had a field day too, as the night heat made the sleeping bag unbearable and my exposed arms were bitten extensively. My feet are all fucked up—grotesquely discolored, swollen, and blistered from the five hour march. The others mock me, christening me Trench Foot.

It is shortly after dawn, and a group of men are waiting outside the hut, ready for work. They all carry machetes, a file for the machete, lunch bags with *pozol*, water mixed with ground corn, and a Zapatista neckerchief, fashioned rebel style. Despite the early hour, they are all jolly, and joke in Tzeltal. Somewhat disheveled, we stagger out and ritualistically shake hands with everyone. The compañeros are giddy with excitement; we are still half asleep.

Today is the first step towards bringing piped water to the village: the topographical study. We will do a geological survey of the territory between the mountain spring and the village. It is, in effect, a feasibility study—will the water arrive by gravitational means at all? For the system to function, there has to be sufficient head, or power in the gravity of the channeled water, to journey the two kilometers over hill and dale to the final destination. The study is to establish the altitude difference (the head) between the water source and the projected reservoir tank in the community.

---

9. A kind of bloodsucking, biting jungle bug that descends in swarms and feeds unrelentingly on humans.

It's a mathematical conundrum, but people with an eye for these things—like Maria—will tell you that if the source is ten meters higher than the village, the piped water will arrive. More recent additions to the water teams, like Praxedis and me, still have to rely on the technical data.

Maria unpacks the transit level, an engineering device that resembles an early-twentieth century tripod camera, to measure the angle from it to poles held by compañeros a hundred meters downhill. With that information, considering the angle and distance, using trigonometry and a pocket calculator, we can calculate the head of water, and figure out what size of piping is needed. If the pressure is too strong for a pipe, it will burst. If the pressure is too weak, it won't travel the distance. More precisely speaking, if the drop in elevation between any point of the pipe system and the spring was to fall below ten meters in the hilly terrain, an air-lock could develop and an expensive valve would have to be installed to prevent a block.

We are all set, but the good Don Sisifo notices the three technicians are still reeling from yesterday's endeavors. Breakfast in his house, he proposes, while the other men go off to prepare the trail through the mountain with their machetes. We retreat to his house.

There is a warm, nesting environment about this simple hut, filled with children, chickens, ducks, cats, and dogs. Don Sisifo pours water upon our hands—a campo cleansing ritual—before we eat. Doña Dolores smiles kindly and remains quiet and receptive to our perceived demands. On a rough table, we are served eggs and beans and tortillas. It tastes absolutely delicious. We eat in silence, humbled, and slightly embarrassed by the family, all standing in corners watching over us, as if to make sure we are completely satisfied. Spartan and clean, the dirt-floor hut is filled with gentle smoke from the open fire and the delicious smell of cooking tortillas. We sip sugary coffee from metal cups. The children gaze upon us with wonder, as if we, as *caxlanes*[10]—that is, outsiders—eat in some extraordinary manner. Doña Dolores is demure and polite, and we reciprocate. Despite a thousand insect bites and little sleep

---

10. *Caxlan* is a catch-all word in Tzeltal and Tsotsil that refers to outsiders, whether they are from other parts of Chiapas, from other parts of Mexico, or from other countries. *Ladinos*, or non-indigenous. The word is sometimes spelled *kaxlan*, or even *jkaxlan*.

(and let's not forget trench foot) we feel ridiculously pampered, our bellies full and sated.

Around 8 AM we set off over the hills and towards the spring, a two kilometer journey. The mud is heavy and the surrounding forest rich and fecund. Up at the spring, we are happy to see that the compas have already made a solid concrete spring box as part of a previous attempt to build a water system here. Water has been walled in at the source to form a well that funnels the liquid into an exit-flow valve. A difficult job, pitting gushing spring water against stone and mortar with the time it takes cement to dry. So we "water techies" are satisfied that we are off to a good start, as two or three days of planned labor have already been done. What's here is a solid wall, a good spring box. It's not how we would have constructed it, but it's obviously appropriate to the site. We measure the flow of the water, a liter every nine seconds—a good and strong flow. Maria takes a water sample in a bottle for chemical and bacteriological tests that will be done back in a clinic in San Cristobal.

Someone has scratched the words "*Agudo* Santa Tomas" into the cement of the wall, after the saint of water. And misspelled it.

"We need to change that," mentions Gordo.

"What? The name of the spring?"

"Well, just the spelling. Although we could change the name too. You don't like Aguado Santa Tomas?"

"No, it's fine," says Praxedis. "But every single spring in the region seems to be called Aguado Santa Tomas."

"So you think we should re-name it?" asks Vicente.

"Sure, if the community wants to change the name, I think it's a good idea," says Praxedis, not elaborating upon his distaste for religious iconography on account of his profoundly atheistic outlook.

The compas confer amongst themselves for a few moments.

"The compas have decided on a proposal for a name," declares Vicente.

Yes?

"'Zapatista Spring.' Because, we are Zapatistas, and you water technicians, you are Zapatistas too."

Well, that was very kind and generous of them.

The spring is situated in a lush bower, surrounded by a dense forest of old-growth trees. The compañeros clear the brush around the spring and then start on the trail where we will dig a trench to bury the pipes. Machete in one hand and a clawed stick to pull back the debris with the other, the campesinos go to work with precision. Gordo is in charge of the measuring tape. As the occasional math teacher in the school, he has, unlike the others, a good grip on measurements. He takes the lead in measuring the path 100 meters at a time through the forest, across gullies, up and down hills, and across streams. He's an outgoing guy and speaks good Spanish, is constantly inquisitive and asks all the right questions. Soon he is calculating the gradation with the transit, and teaching other campesinos how to do it. The shining sun, the hum of activity, and productive work, informs the pleasant nature of our activities. In the broadest pedagogical sense, the compas are already doing it for themselves.

We return to Roberto Arenas, heavy footed and silent in the late afternoon. Quieted, not because we are bored or listless, but because the work was exhausting and the symphony of the jungle and the mountains has filled our heads with word and song. We don't need conversation now.

And so to the river for a much-needed bath. The wide, green river flows by through a tropical jungle corridor and it is a delight to wade in and swim.

"Mind the snakes and the crocodiles!" warns a nearby compa, and we laugh, only a mite nervously. On the other bank, a gaggle of women wash clothes on rocks, surrounded by naked children. The scene is one of pastoral tranquility and waves of stillness wash over us. Life hasn't changed much around these mountains for a long time and it seems people like it that way.

Sleep comes easily, as I rearrange the hammock, using my keffiyeh as a kind of mini-mosquito net (tricks of the trade for long-term jungle activists) and the bugs don't get at me so easily tonight. As a content slumber engulfs me, I'm satisfied that this water project will go well, the community is motivated, and we can do it.

Maria sets off early the next day with Don Sisifo to survey the community and to make a detailed map we'll use to design the pipeline. She will visit each of the twenty-three houses to talk to the occupants about the project, and will take the opportunity to meet the women and ask them of their specific water needs.

Accompanied by Vicente and Alfredo, the two responsables who will be in charge of overseeing the ongoing maintenance of the water system, Praxedis and I are dispatched up the mountain to fortify the spring box. Machete in hand, we hack through the thick undergrowth all the way to the source of the fresh water. It's September, the rainy season has been an abundant one, and the mud is so deep that we are sometimes struggling up to our knees.

The clearing at the spring is a truly enchanting place, filled with a dizzying array of plants, trees, and animal life. This virgin water, running anciently and mysteriously out of the deep earth, is gorgeous and cool to touch. We are surrounded by the powerful perfume of feral nature blooming and blossoming. The pungent odor of decay and growth, of lush ecosystems and regeneration permeates the air.

We begin to dam the spring, in order to stop leaves and debris from entering the capitation tank and blocking the pipes. We can also use heavy rocks from the surrounding area to construct a solid wall. One of the compas strips off and wades into the water digging up half-submerged rocks. I scout the area and notice, almost invisible in the dense foliage, an encampment. Tables and chairs and posts hued from branches and forest wood around a campfire pit. Now it is overgrown and obviously derelict, but my imagination bounds. I'm certain it's a guerrilla encampment, used by a group of transient Zapatistas. Even though there has not been any combat since the early days of 1994, rumors still abound about the presence of EZLN guerrillas in the mountains. Hidden from public view, they have become the stuff of village lore. Have I stumbled across something I was not meant to see? Of course, beside a freshwater spring, hidden deep below the forest canopy is an ideal location for a clandestine camp. I cast my gaze around and notice a variety of wooden structures that look vaguely familiar from diagrams in Che Guevara's Manual For Guerrilla warfare. It seems a magical place, filled with clandestinity and memories, resonant of dreams and struggle.

"Vicente!" I call. "What's this encampment over here?"

He looks at me curiously, "This is where we held a ceremony on Santa Tomas Day, the day to bless the water..."

That was a little disappointing.

But it is not like the compas are hiding their affiliation. As we work, Vicente and Alfredo, little by little, begin to open up and chat to us, telling us a little of their lives and tales.

We break for a mid-morning snack of *matz*, a corn porridge drink popular in these parts. I remember first trying it a few years ago when I began working in the zone, and almost vomited. Other volunteers did vomit. Just took a swig of the heavy, ground down corn and water, and, straight up, vomited. It's slightly fermented flavor makes it an acquired taste, which I think I have acquired now. It leaves a bitter taste in your mouth and lots of residue, but it is filling and, as the compas never tire of telling you wherever you go in these canyons—matz gives you strength.

Vicente is a young man in his early twenties, married with two little kids. Although short in stature, he appears sturdy and strong, muscles bulging everywhere, and exudes good health. Must be the matz.

His family came from further down the valley because there was no land left in his community for the next generation. He, like most of the landless youngsters there, joined the Zapatistas to fight for new land. He tells us how, on January 1st 1994, his unit descended upon the town of Ocosingo, and fought the military. They lost some compañeros in the battle.

"My brother Jorge fell," he relates, and falls into silence, ruminating upon his dead sibling.

"Sorry," we say.

Alfredo, who is a couple of years older than Vicente, and has a couple of kids more, participated in the takeover of Ocosingo too. The battle of the market a few days later was one the worst in the whole war. Dozens of compañeros and civilians were killed after the army surrounded them in the town market. He doesn't say much about it.

"It was very hard," says Alfredo, "but we managed to escape out the back way. Many of our compañeros were not so lucky."

Since the conversation has taken a dark turn, I change the subject.

"Are you two related?" I noticed when they introduced themselves, that one's name was Lopez Santiz, and the other Santiz Lopez.

"We are second cousins."

They begin to explain but it gets complicated. A lot of Lopez and Santiz marrying each other and it seems almost everyone in the community is connected by family in some way or the other. I suppose that explains the one-big-happy-family atmosphere all around.

Back to work, the supply of water gushing out of the exit pipe is plentiful and we hook up the connections with a flood-gate valve, a globe valve, and a metal ring to connect the supply to the first roll of the PVC pipe. We do everything slowly and carefully, wrapping all the parts with tape; if everything is done well this water system should work suitably for twenty-five years. However, there are a few problems with the materials—the floodgate valve is slightly malfunctioning. Because of budget restrictions we had to buy a cheap model, and this has proven a bad call. Vicente curses the device, blaming it on sub-standard Chinese engineering. I am surprised that this particular prejudice reached even here, the heart of the Lacandon Jungle. Praxedis considers the defective piece from a different perspective.

"Probably forced prison labor."

Nevertheless, it functions, and we decide to leave it be. And so the spring is ready to start feeding a pipe network. All we need to do is get the pipes here.

Back at base, all the men have gathered outside the school for a water workshop. We invite them in and as they ask a few questions I notice that, though guarded, they are slightly less shy towards us techies—a good sign.

Maria begins a short presentation on water and health, and after a while mentions that it would be useful to have the women present for this too. She points out that it would be good to include them in the process, not least because water is a primary concern of the women. The men talk amongst themselves in Tzeltal and eventually Gordo turns to us and explains that the women are busy in the kitchen at the moment, but they will participate in the next stage.

Not wanting to push it, Maria continues explaining the details of the water system, basic engineering, and finally, that the cost of the system will be covered by the project, but each individual household will have to pay for its own tap-stand, about 100 pesos, or $10 US. The project pays for public tap-stands, but private ones cost. The thinking behind the strategy is that people will take more care of the system if they have paid a little money into it.

Gordo has translated all, but at this point, a problem arises. A heated discussion ensues between the assembled men, but we are not privy to the details.

"The compas are discussing," is all Gordo will tell us, although it is obviously about the cost, as the word *tak'in*—money—is bandied about a lot.

We are witness to how the indigenous Zapatistas make decisions and come to agreement: the argument flows back and forward in the gravelly clack of the Tzeltal tongue for half an hour. Almost everybody has their say, and eventually they come to a decision by consensus. Everybody is on board.

"The compas say it is all fine," says Gordo. And that is it—we have no idea what they were discussing or why, but we are told its all OK. I suppose in the same manner that we tell the compas everything is fine with the topographical study and they shouldn't worry about it. There is a distinct problem in communication and we have not quite yet bridged the gap. It is something we need to work on.

Early afternoon, we pack up the transit level in preparation for the long trek back to La Garrucha, and from there, home to San Cristobal. We are off to write up the feasibility study, make the basic engineering calculations, and order the necessary materials. We return in a week's time with a truckload of pipes and cement and taps. In the meantime, with the limited amount of hoes and shovels available, the villagers will start digging a two kilometer ditch, about seventy centimeters deep and fifteen centimeters wide.

As we pack, the men hand over the money for personal taps in their homesteads. It feels really harsh to accept cash from these desperately poor families. Feeling a little like Sheriff of Nottingham's bailiffs, with our bag of collected money, we bid farewell to all and sunder and set off over the mountain one more time, accompanied by two young compañeros. I think if any would-be Robin Hoods from the community intercepted us in the hills, I would happily hand the money back over.

It rained heavily most of last night, so it is another torturous mountain hike along muddy trails. As we march I notice that the last crop of corn is cut and nobody is replanting. Nothing is growing now, our guides explain, so the people are waiting for the weather to improve. The sun is too hot during the day and the rain torrential during the night, which is very unusual for this time of year. Global warming, we surmise, fucking up the environment.

"Are the compañeros worried about this year's crop?" we ask.

"Yeah. Every year we worry about the crop," the compas respond. "This year more than usual."

Once more the midday sun beats down on us unceasingly and there is little cover. Our boots stick in the ankle deep mud and progress is slow. All around us the scenic countryside, but we never look up from our boots for fear of falling over in the mud. We really have no precise idea how long the journey is—maybe ten kilometers?—because distance is measured here in the mountains by walking time. We make it in a little under five and a half hours, so we feel satisfied. It is brutal terrain and we make it, slightly quicker than the previous time.

Around dusk, we see the welcoming lights of the village La Garrucha beckoning us like returned prodigal sons. Electricity! We trudge into the caracol and the warmth of the welcome from the resident peace campers. It's a homecoming of sorts, and makes us feel relieved. Oh, to rest our weary legs! But not so for our guides—the two young compas who accompanied us from Roberto Arenas turn back. It is 6 PM, and they are heading home, another long hike back, this time in darkness over the mountain.

Subversive Activities

Our study reveals it will be a model project with few complications. There are no brake pressure tanks or bridges to construct, we will lay two kilometers of one-inch PVC tube, running to a large 13,000 liter concrete tank that will be situated at the community's highest point. It will have two lead-off lines serving all twenty-three houses in the hamlet, as well as a few public tap-stands.

Getting the necessary materials to the community is a challenge. A jungle dirt road does pass near the community, but on the other side of the wide, unbridged Jataté River. If we can deliver the goods to the riverside, the community will have to transport them over the river in a canoe, a hazardous task.

Another obstacle is the Mexican army camp and the roadblock at El Abismo, about three miles from the potential drop off point. The army could confiscate the supplies. The people transporting the materials could be detained. Foreigners with them could be deported for being in the "conflict zone" or deemed to be "subversives" working with the Zapatistas.

Maria, Praxedis, and I are most definitely subversive, in any State-defined sense of the word, but if engaging in plumbing is a subversive activity to be prohibited then it makes the Mexican State look pretty fascist. This is the political space we operate in: always at risk of detention or deportation, but slipping through the cracks.

So we have a cunning plan. A ten-ton truck has been hired from the construction materials dealer and they've arranged for two drivers to deliver the goods. The drivers have little notion of where they are going except that it's to a community in the jungle—six or seven hours drive from the town of Ocosingo. Praxedis and I will accompany them for most of the journey to give them directions. Maria will come along a few days later in a separate vehicle with more gear.

One element we hadn't factored into our brilliant plan was the state of inebriation of our two delivery guys. The arrangement was to meet at the gas station just outside Ocosingo at 5 AM. Praxedis and I arrive early, having left San Cristobal by public transport around midnight. Sure enough, the big truck is there, filled to capacity with bulky plastic tubes, cement bags, and tools. The two men are fast asleep in the cabin, snoring like rhinoceroses. We tap on the window and they wake with a start. Introductions are made and our two lads—Oliver, the fat one, and Estanley, the skinny one—are very friendly, although the smell of liquor on their breath could knock you over.

"Let's get this show on the road!" says the chubby one, starting the engine.

"I'm right with you, Oly," says Estanley, the co-pilot.

"You sure you're OK to drive? Seems you lads had a bit of a party last night."

"I can drive," offers Praxedis.

"No. Only we can drive. Boss's order. And don't worry, we've slept off our drunkenness. Now we're just hungover!"

Fuck. I pull Praxedis aside. They are a dishevelled mess, but we need to get that gear to the community today. The thought of waiting another day is unbearable. And it could get costly—we are renting the truck by the hour.

"Let's see how they handle it. I can take over if they're too fucked up."

I squeeze into the cabin between the two boys and Praxedis climbs into the back and sits amongst the tubing and cement.

The lads seem to be sobering up. They are very friendly, relating their night's activities with enthusiasm. It seems that they arrived in Ocosingo around midnight, left the truck and materials at the gas station (unguarded—thanks lads!) and re-located to a local bar called Osama's Cave—a seedy, dangerous cantina frequented by guttersnipes, desperados, and drug addicts, and populated by working girls—pretty typical for these small towns. Estanley waxes lyrically on the late-night prowess of one Maricela from El Salvador, while Oly got his rocks off with someone from Honduras. Both migrants, apparently, earning a little cash on their long way up north to the USA.

How much did they charge, I ask, intrigued.

"500 pesos a pop," informs Oly.

"More than we get paid for this job!" snickers Estanly. "But worth every centavo."

Both fall into a loud bout of non-infectious chortling.

And are all the girls foreigners? Migrants?

"Yeah, all sluts from Salvador, Honduras, Nicaragua."

"Although there were a couple of *indios* too," says Estanley.

"Yeah, fat and ugly Chiapaneco indios. Nobody bothered with them, though. Who wants to fuck an indio?"

There is nothing unusual about the men's racist and sexist commentary. It's all too prevalent in Chiapas, and it is always tiresome.

I change the subject. "Have you driven around these parts before?"

"The Lacandon Jungle? No, never. They tell us the roads are a disaster and that they're crawling with bandits and armed Zapatista *guerrilleros*. It is a fucked-up place. Nobody else would do the delivery so they were left with us two mad bastards!"

Another round of boisterous, cackling laughter ensues.

"You don't have to worry about the Zapatistas," I assure them.

But these two lads have a different impression of the rebels.

They are two working men, *mestizos*—mixed race—from Tuxtla, the state capital of Chiapas and are not at all informed. Not unusual for urban mestizos, they have a racist attitude towards the indigenous and consider themselves superior. Of the Zapatistas they know next to nothing, except that a communist mestizo called Marcos has got them all riled up and they want to burn down Tuxtla and everyone in it. Estanley and Oly are pro-government, pro-army, and all for wiping out the "Indian subversives."

Oh dear. These lads are in for a surprise. I feel less guilty about not being totally straight about this delivery. Still, I'm thinking, they should have no problem getting through the military checkpoint at El Abismo with their attitude. The soldiers will love them.

The drivers think that we are with an international NGO with a link to the Catholic Church, delivering charity to a poor indigenous community that lost everything in a flood.

There's an ornament of the Virgin of Guadalupe stuck to the dashboard, so I think the Catholic angle would go down well with the lads. It does.

"May the Virgin bless you. It is a gift from God Almighty that foreigners come to Mexico to help the poor," says Estanley, maudlin.

I'm glad Praxedis isn't here to hear this shite—his militant atheism would not withstand such provocation.

As we leave the paved road and start bouncing along the rocky, winding road to the jungle, the men begin to get nervous. At one particularly scary curve—a precipitous fifty-yard drop on one side—the truck does indeed tilt dangerously towards the abyss. Estanley reaches for the half-empty bottle of Pox liquor stashed under the seat and takes a swig, "Jesus, Mary, and Joseph, that was close!"

Oly takes a swig too. "Cheers, to the graveyard!"

Praxedis is banging on the roof.

"Let me drive!" he shouts.

But Oly wont let him. "No, no, too dangerous. You need to know this truck well to get through this fucking treacherous road. And you never know what's around the next corner."

And it's true. Never mind about his nervous disposition, Oly can drive. It is the idea of the Lacandon Jungle that is freaking him out. For these guys this place is dark and mysterious and filled with potential enemies. Here there are monsters, a desert of solitude, or heart of darkness. I reflect how it is always a relief for me and Praxedis to arrive in rebel territory, to be away from the teeming, overcrowded towns. For these men from Tuxtla, though, the lair of the Zapatistas is a fearsome place.

"And the Zapatistas have never grabbed you?" asks Estanley, fascinated that a foreigner would work quite contentedly in these badlands. "I have heard that they tie outsiders to trees to be attacked by bees for days on end!"

"Only drunk outsiders. To teach them a lesson," I tell poor petrified Estanley. He takes another gulp of his bottle of Tiburon Pox. Pox is this highly potent and horribly dangerous mentholated spirit that is as useful for cleaning car engines as it is for getting plastered. And it makes you blind of course. People like Estanley seem to love it for some reason.

I relocate to the top of the truck to join Praxedis for the last leg of the journey. It's not that the lads' sexist, racist, nationalistic, and dim-witted buffoonery is getting to me—they are quite pleasant men despite all that—it is the hideous smell of their constant farting. Pox-ridden farts, springing from their fetid bowels, is just too much. They are not bad men, just a bit ignorant (maybe a few months in a Zapatista guerrilla re-education camp would do them a world of good.)[11] Anyhow, I reckon I am probably safer on top of the truck where I can jump ship before we plunge over the edge, into the abyss.

Nestled amongst rolls of pipe and cement bags, we enjoy a picaresque and exciting journey, as we bump along the rough track. When we arrive at the little community situated just before the El Abismo encampment and roadblock, we bang on the roof of the cabin to stop the truck.

"Here we disembark, and the community will meet you on the side of the road about half an hour down the valley, OK?"

"Side of the road?" repeats the driver, puzzled. "No village or community drop-off?"

It's the other side of the river, we explain, they are going to ferry the materials across the river.

"Holy virgin! Can't one of you stay with us? We could get lost! And how will we know them?"

---

11. A joke. There are no re-education camps here. Marcos is more Gandhi than Pol Pot.

"They will know you," we assure them. "They are waiting there. You are the only truck full of plumbing materials trundling along this road today. In fact, you are possibly the only traffic along this dirt-track today, so it will be fine!"

Off they go, Oly and Estanley, nervous and uncertain, but their fears unfounded. We are confident their innocence will see them through the military checkpoint. After all, they are just a couple of delivery guys dropping off the materials.

Alberto, a compa from Roberto Arenas is here waiting for us. He is a friendly young man, and it is a relief to talk to someone whose topic of conversation does not revolve around Pox, whores, and the Virgin Mary. He has a *paliacate*[12] tied around one eye like a pirate, as if he had a little accident.

"Is your eye OK?" asks Praxedis. "Did you get a sting or something stuck in it?"

"No problem, Don Praxedis, it is fine," he says, deferentially.

Alberto will lead us the long way via a series of mountain paths, around the Army encampment, to the community. The problem is that this is a PRI-ista hamlet—a pro-government community—and we will have to cross their land. We are relying on the good faith that they, as poor campesinos with no axe to grind, will not block our passage or bother to report the presence of two caxlanes wandering around the backwoods to the nearby military camp. We think that such a scenario would be more trouble than is worth for them.

Alberto assures us that our passage will be fine, as the community is not hostile. We set off on the muddy path, passing through the small community—a splattering of stick huts—greeting the local people cordially as we pass.

A couple of young men loiter at the edge of the hamlet.

"Where are you going?" they ask us, surprised by our appearance.

"To Roberto Arenas," explains Alberto. "These are water engineers."

"Oh," the PRI-istas reply, as if unconcerned. Maybe they are weighing up the odds—to stop us and report our presence to their allies, the military, or to say nothing. In the end, it seems their allegiance to the military is not so urgent—they don't detain us, or tie us to a tree, and so we have safe passage.

This, dear reader, demonstrates the cat and mouse game

---

12. A paliacate is a red neckerchief commonly worn by Zapatista's and supporters.

involved in building solidarity and Zapatista autonomy—or to put it more blandly, in delivering drinkable water to rebel communities. We have safe passage—or so we thought. It turns out to be a difficult four-hour hike to Roberto Arenas, because, as the compa Alberto laments, the track has disappeared, overgrown, reclaimed by the forest. And we still have to cross the river. An old hammock bridge—twenty-meters long, hand-made from wire, rope, and planks, and perilously decrepit—spans the raging Jataté white waters. It's something straight off a Hollywood movie. Pulling on my Indiana Jones cap, I cross first, slowly, gripping the wire handrail tenuously. The wooden slats are rotten and missing in places, and I place my foot gently on each existing one, holding on to the rusty wires for dear life. With the waters raging below me and the wind howling in my face—crash!—I fall through the bridge and find myself dangling over this manic, churning river. My grip on the wire supports are my only saving grace. Fuck!

Would it be romantic to be the first water project team martyr? "Amateur Plumber Drowns on Way to Work!" I imagine the headline in the local paper. But alas, it is not to be. I manage to pull myself up, less glamorously than Indiana Jones but I will take what I can get here in this desolate, melancholic wilderness. It is probably the closest I will get in all my life to reckless, superhero abandon. I scurry across the rest of the damaged slats, reckoning that the shorter time I spend on this rickety, rotting foot bridge the less chance I have of being killed by it. Good philosophy. Praxedis and Alberto both run across, fleet-footed and light, and make it safely across. That Alberto does so with such balanced one-eyed poise makes the feat even more impressive.

The rest of the hike is dull by comparison but still we have to fight our way through rough shrub and bush for hours, and we lack even a machete to cut a trail. Occasionally it is thick forest, jungle even, with huge fallen old tree trunks blocking our way, and we have to climb over or burrow under them. It's a brutal journey, and we are covered head-to-toe with cuts and bruises. With some relief we chance upon a clear path and saunter the last hour towards Roberto Arenas.

And finally there's that familiar little clearing in front of the wide river, the few houses scattered around the place and the placid schoolhouse. Home sweet home.

Don Sisifo comes over to greet us.

"How was the journey?"

"Piece of cake," says Praxedis, nonchalantly.

"And the materials, did they arrive?"

"Yes," answers Don Sisifo, nonchalantly. "More or less. The men were drunk. We were going to lock them up for their own good."

That must have terrified poor Estanley and Oly, I thought. Their fears nearly justified!

We eat in Don Sisifo's kitchen and Doña Dolores smiles shyly, proudly serving bitter coffee, remembering we don't take sugar and thinking we must be quite mad not to enjoy a little sweetness.

A meeting is convened as the evening grows dark, and again all the men gather in the shadows of the schoolroom. The materials did indeed arrive, and are safely stashed on the other side of the river, guarded by two compas. Tomorrow they will begin ferrying everything across the Jataté. Everyone seems a bit nervous about that crossing, and there is something else...

Among the dozens of rolls of pipe and the sixty bags of cement and the valves and taps and wire and the thousand bits and pieces that make up a water system, something important has been forgotten. We go through the list carefully: bolt-cutters, check; metal saw, check; pliers, check; hand-level, check; pipe-level, check; hammer, check; lump-hammer, check; trowels, check; plains, check; lead-weight, check; plastic mixing buckets, wrenches, measuring tape, shovels, check, check, check, check; picks... Shit. We have neglected to pack the picks. Fuck. The extreme impoverishment of this community is reflected by the fact that their whole supply of tools comes to about half a dozen good, working shovels and a few picks between the twenty-five workers. How can they dig a two kilometer ditch without enough picks or shovels?

Praxedis and I are deeply embarrassed by our mistake, but we have a plan! Maria is coming up in a few days time. Can we get a message to her? We ask the assembly. A long conversation in Tzeltal ensues. Well, they explain, we can radio down to La Garrucha, send a message from there to San Cristobal. It's complicated and uncertain. In the end, a compañero volunteers to undertake the long journey to San Cristobal. Like most of his fellow communards, he has never been that far away from the village and despite taking on the mantle of a great expedition, he is willing to give it a go. It is in the ensuing discussion that we discover that it is only a couple of the older community members who have been to San Cristobal, and quite historically, that was to occupy it in the bold armed uprising of Jan 1st, 1994. Don Job and the other elder who had participated in the rising blush demurely and the rest of us are delighted to hear their story. "It was a cold, dark, stormy night…"

Outside in the still-murky jungle night, horses move about chomping, while dogs, pigs, chickens, ducks, and turkeys lurk. Frogs hop around on the ground, mingling with snakes and scorpions. A plague of chaquistas and mosquitoes linger. All is as it should be in the turbulent Lacandon night.

Ferry Across the Jataté

We need to get all the materials stored before it starts raining. They are currently on the other side of the river, watched by some compas who spent the night guarding them. Protecting them from whom is not certain, as the little dirt track is almost always deserted, except for a very occasional military vehicle or the daily early morning bus to Ocosingo, and absolutely nothing passes by night.

Such is the excitement about the water project that the whole community treks down to the river on the muddy bank waiting for the materials to cross over. It allows us our first glimpse of the women en masse in their traditional colorful dresses. They don't talk to us, the caxlanes, and shy glances aside, concern themselves mostly with the numerous kids abounding, and quiet contemplation.

"Praxedis! Why have these people gathered here?"

"I guess nothing much happens in these parts."

All of us watch the powerful river churn by. It's not the Amazon or the Congo but its twenty-meters wide and raging. We are in the midst of the rainy season—so much rain! It falls intermittingly, with great force, so suddenly, heavily. And in its wake, the mud; mud up to ones ankles.

Watching the river flow by for hours on end becomes mesmeric and fascinating—and I begin to understand why this is a point of convergence for the remote, jungle community.

Ferrying the materials across the Jataté River is an art unto itself. Using a twenty-foot canoe, hand-carved from a great old tree, one compa stands at the back, steering with a rough oar, while another kneels down at the front, rowing. It is a delicate operation and the canoe, although an artisan work of some measure, is well worn from too many crossings and seems dangerously low in the water. The currents are strong due to the increased rain and the river is swelled to capacity. Don Sisifo takes the helm and begins the long slog of transporting the materials, including some sixty bags of cement, bit by bit, across the expanse of jungle river.

The heavy canoe strains under the weight of the men and four bags of cement for each journey. But this rustic old vessel is good for the job. With minute precision, Captain Sisifo maneuvers the canoe down the rapids, across the swells, and up the eddies of this powerful river. It is a remarkable piece of riverman-ship, Sisifo at the stern with his long oar, Vicente kneeling in the bow. Crossing again and again, sweating and fighting the current all afternoon—two dozen times in total—all the while hoping that it won't rain and wet the cement bags and render them useless.

Meanwhile on the other bank, we porter the material half a kilometer over dirt paths to a storehouse on the far side of the village. The heavier pieces, like 100 meter rolls of one-inch PVC tubing, or 50-kilo bags of cement, are miraculously carried by men using mecapal head straps. This is heavy-duty hauling, the men slipping around in the mud with fifty kilos of cement balanced precariously on their backs. The storehouse is located in a room of the old manager's (*finqueros*) house—a fine, though crumbling, old building on top of a hill overlooking the valley and the river bed. It's the only stone building in the whole community of earthen-floored, grass- or corrugated-iron-roofed huts. It sits at the highest point in the hamlet, and is possibly the only area that won't be flooded when the river breaks its banks, as it has done in the past. It's the one place guaranteed to be dry, so the pile of cement bags will be safe there. It is also the location we've chosen for the main water tank, so it's useful to have the materials nearby.

We check the inventory and it appears that all the materials made it. The truck began the ten-hour road journey yesterday at dawn, and we carried the last cement bag into the old stone house as night fell the next day. We have not even started construction and it's already taken so much time and effort—these people work hard to build their community.

"*Poco a poco*," says Don Sisifo, little by little, reflecting on the slow, patient process.

He seems very pleased that the materials have arrived and this water system is becoming a reality. It is like, after a lifetime of spoiled expectations and disappointments, actually seeing the cement and pipes here before him fills his heart with joy. I feel like giving him a little embrace, but one would never do such a sappy thing with an upright man such as he.

Praxedis and I retire back to the schoolhouse at dusk. The village seems deserted except for the sound of the children play-marching around in the distance, chanting Zapatista slogans. The sadness of the dirt-floor schoolhouse resonates, empty but for a few rustic wooden desks, a ragged map of the world, and a chalk board with the remains of a short list of names written on it. All that is left are a few dusty books on a shelf, and a forlorn compass. But mostly, it is the sense of interruption, like the school stopped functioning one day and everything is in limbo.

Saturday night in Roberto Arenas. The immense, starry sky over the valley and the natural silence is overwhelming. In the distance, we can make out various houses illumined by flickering candle light. We are warm in the bosom of the valley by the river, and it would be perfectly tranquil except our candlelight is attracting a bad crowd, and we are being devoured by swarms of chaquistas and mosquitoes.

A voice in the darkness calls out to Praxedis.

"*Sí?*"

"May we enter?" requests a voice in the blackness.

Three compañeros enter shyly and we invite them to sit around the candlelight. An awkward silence ensues.

Gordo, the outgoing one of the group, begins:

"We have come to talk to you."

"OK," says Praxedis and another two minutes of silence passes.

In a decisive act of social bonding, I crack out a packet of cigarettes and offer them around. The three compañeros accept them gratefully. It soon becomes clear that the other two are overcome with intense shyness and speak no Spanish. They whisper to Gordo for a few minutes in Tzeltal, and then point at us.

"You are the first caxlanes to ever visit our community," says Gordo. "The compañeros are very pleased you came. They wanted to come to welcome you."

The two silent ones smile and nod their heads in unison. It's very touching.

We smile back and say "*jocolawal*" — thank you, in Tzeltal.

"Do you come from the United States?" Gordo asks of me.

"No," I say, "Ireland."

Gordo looks confused.

"Europe," I offer.

He nods, and explains to the others. They look disappointed.

"The compañeros thought you came from the United States."

"I'm sorry, no."

"And what country does your compañero come from?"

Now this is the thing. Praxedis may be a bit of a quiet fellow, but he is most definitely Mexican and speaks with a very pronounced Mexico City accent. Why is the compañero asking me, the non-Spanish speaker, about Praxedis?! I am taken aback.

"He is from Mexico! A *chilango*!"[13]

Gordo turns quite excitedly to his companions and reveals to them this gem of information! They discuss this at length and then turn to Praxedis, somewhat uncertain.

"You are Mexican?! We thought you were from another country!"

"Well, DF does seem like another country from here, it's true," says Praxedis, and everybody laughs.

"Why did you think he is from another country?" I ask.

"Well, he is not like the other mestizos we have seen."

True enough, the small provincial town of Ocosingo — probably the extent of these campesinos travels — would not have many inhabitants like Praxedis, with his tattoos, punky-look and pronounced chilango accent.

And so the conversation begins and we end up talking deep

---

13. Native of Mexico City.

into the night, with Gordo acting as informal moderator between the rest of us.

The two quiet ones are introduced—they are brothers, Ricardo and Enrique, and it must be noted that these two look completely different from everyone else here in the community. For a start they have beards, while most of the other men, typical for indigenous, have no facial hair. They are several inches taller than everyone else and resemble Galician fishermen, perhaps from a few centuries ago. Neither has a word of Spanish, but they emanate a natural friendliness and warmth. We share cigarettes and talk—we in Spanish, they in Tzeltal. Although we don't understand much, it's enough to laugh and smile while enjoying the hushed darkness.

After discussing the price of our boots and how much plane tickets cost from Ireland, the talk turns to the United States, the work situation up north, and how to get there. They know people who have tried to migrate without papers, without success, but they all entertain ideas of going there anyhow, somehow.

"What of the Zapatista struggle to stay and fight for a better world here?" asks Praxedis. The three campesinos speak in Tzeltal among themselves for what seems a long time.

Eventually Gordo turns to us and says, "We can do both. Work up north, and fight down here. But there is no money here, so we must seek work up there."

He goes on to describe how $3 a day is the best they can hope for working locally in Chiapas as hired farm-workers. In the United States, he says—his face lighting up—compañeros can make $10 an hour, as much as a $100 a day!

"Sure," he explains, "we get by working on our milpas here, growing corn to feed our families and we can survive. But... [Gordo points at my black punk-rock boots] how can we afford anything more if we have no money?"

The pressure on youths and young men and women to make the dangerous and uncertain trip north is greater as the government's neo-liberal policies undermine the traditional peasant economy. Imports of mass-produced corn from the US, undermines the local market for this basic good, and campesinos are literally forced off the land because they are priced out. Some farmers change their focus away from corn, and plant cash crops like coffee or start palm-oil plantations for biofuel, but with the perennial shortage of good land, a sizeable portion of the youth are forced to migrate. The Zapatistas counteract this pattern by imploring campesinos to stay and fight, to take over more land and to work together collectively to produce more efficiently through farmers' cooperatives.

"*No hay tak'in*—there's no money here," laments Gordo. "We can't afford to buy anything."

To labor the point he reaches over and picks up an old Walkman I have by my side. It is a real piece of shit I picked up back home after someone threw it away.

"How does this work?" he asks.

After spending a while in the indigenous communities in the Lacandon region, one begins to see patterns emerge. Like how sometimes our presence—as caxlanes—represents a disruptive influence in these rural communities. Even though we come with good intentions, invited to be here and participating in valuable projects requested by the people themselves, our presence still has a powerful impact. Compañeros up and down the canyons or in the jungle always ask: How come you can travel the world, have all this electrical equipment, fancy clothes and boots, expensive sleeping bags, etc., when we, as campesinos, have none of this?

"Do you work harder than us?" Gordo asks rhetorically.

No, of course we don't.

Praxedis tries to explain it in terms of capitalist inequalities, but I can see that the language he uses is going over Gordo's head. He gets neo-liberalism, exploitation, and class war, but looks confused when Praxedis tries to explain surplus value and means of production—I must confess to being a bit lost myself.

Gordo asks him to elaborate.

Praxedis likes to make an effort at popular education with the compas. Political theory is his forte, and I have seen some compañeros in other communities really take to Praxedis's political lessons. And sometimes, like tonight, they bomb. He sees it as part of his duty as an anarchist to share his political theory with the Zapatista cadre. How else, he insists, will they ever hear these important ideas?

Praxedis comes from Mexico City and his political outlook comes from the radical urban milieu there. The anarchist movement in Mexico City is (relatively) sizeable and broad enough to have several competing tendencies and factions who seem to be eternally at loggerheads. Praxedis's group have made it a priority to be actively involved in autonomous and popular movements as their praxis for building an anarchist platform. For them political solidarity is inserting oneself as an anarchist in the movement with the aim of pushing it further, while sharing the common goal of the specific campaign—broadly considered the *especifismo* tendency. Praxedis's outlook is premised in the idea that people who have different political ideas can work together, and paradoxically, unity is discovered in diversity. Most of all, this kind of anarchist practice prioritizes movement building over political correctness and eschews promoting a "correct line" like other, more fundamentalist, practitioners on the left.

Proselytizing in the indigenous communities is problematic: while the ideology and the aspirations of an anarchist may carry many similarities with the struggle of the Zapatistas, it is the cultural divide between the city and the countryside that seems a wider chasm to cross. The life experiences of the indigenous peasant and the urban mestizo are worlds apart.

In an attempt to bridge the gap in understanding, in theory and practice, I relate the long history of uprising and armed struggle against occupation and "bad government" in my country, Ireland—and this comes as quite a surprise to Gordo.

"There is an armed struggle against bad government in your country?" he repeats as if to make sure he heard right, and when he relays this back to the others, they are clearly perturbed.

"We thought only poor people like us had to fight, not rich gringo caxlanes like you..."

Interactions like this don't bring us any closer, they just consolidate the idea that there is such a huge distance to cross in international solidarity. It begins to resemble a never-ending task that cannot ever be realized, a Sisyphean endeavor.

Outsiders are often drawn to the Zapatistas through the eloquent pen of Subcomandante Marcos and recognize their own struggles in his exquisite words. These communiqués swirled around the globe in the mid-1990s, as Internet-savvy supporters employed new technologies with great effectiveness to circulate the rebel texts. The reality on the ground was of course far different. Many European and US radicals came to Chiapas with great

expectations only to be disappointed by the authoritarian, patriarchal, and conservative movement they encountered at the base.
For those activists, the gap between the image of the Zapatista
struggle created by Marcos's words and the actuality in the communities was a bridge in itself to cross.

In this volume, I am attempting to portray the Zapatistas as
they are, at the grassroots, beyond the mythologizing of Marcos
and the public face of the rebellion. As it did for many others, the
content of the myriad communiqués and letters resonated power-
fully in the political work I was participating in in Europe. Zapatista discourse on autonomy, diversity, resistance to power, and
neo-liberalism reflected a political reality confronted at the center
of the world systems as well as the peripheries. However, it was not
my political background in autonomous and anarchist circles in
Europe that helped me relate to the situation within the Zapatista
communities. What was far more helpful in enabling me to understand the reality in Chiapas was experiences with other campesino struggles in different parts of Latin America, time spent with
revolutionary groups in Nicaragua, Guatemala, and Colombia. In

these scenarios, ideology or theory takes a backseat to the daily exigencies of the struggle for basic survival.

Surely no volume on the Zapatistas is complete without quoting at least one poetic epistle from Subcomandante Marcos! I try to avoid using Marcos's rose-tinted prose to illuminate the Zapatista reality, but this one passage from a communiqué attributed to the Clandestine Committee, but clearly written by Marcos, expresses the perplexing and sometimes contradictory nature of encountering Zapatismo at its base. This sentiment really resonates, I discover, having dug ditches for years with the Zapatistas.

> Zapatismo is not a new political ideology or a rehash of old ideologies. Zapatismo is nothing. It doesn't exist. It only serves as a bridge, to cross from one side to the other. So everyone fits within Zapatismo, everyone who wants to cross from one side to the other. Everyone has his or her own side and other side. There are no universal recipes, lines, strategies, tactics, laws, rules, or slogans. There is only a desire: to build a better world, that is, a new world.[14]

14. Cited from Luis Hernandez Navarro, *Zapatismo Today, Five Views From the Bridge*. Americas Program, Interhemispheric, Resource Centre (IRC) January 2004.

II.

Trench Warfare

"Solidarity requires that one enter into the situation of those with whom one is in solidarity, it is a radical posture." — Paulo Freire, *Pedagogy of the Oppressed*

The Work Begins

It's 5:15 AM, and I can hear voices in the darkness. Disconcerted, I take a moment to remember where I am. I can't be awake at this early hour returning from a club or party—the nightclub scene deep in the Lacandon Rainforest being somewhat lacking—so, yes, I must be working on a water project again. Praxedis is up already, busy doing his exercises outside the schoolhut door.

"Have you made some coffee for me, yet?" I ask, facetiously.

"Fuck off, lazybones. Make it yourself," replies the ridiculously athletic and jolly-at-this-unearthly-hour anarchist from Mexico City.

It's now 5:20 AM. I am probably the last person out of bed in the whole community. I can hear people active all around the valley in the crepuscular dawn: preparing tortillas, chopping wood. There are children laughing, babies crying, dogs barking. The little huts dotted around the horizon glow with soft fires. It's noticeably quiet in the absence of cars, machinery, and electronic devices.

I stumble over to our makeshift kitchen and am pleasantly surprised to discover that Praxedis was lying. There's a glowing wood fire, coffee and eggs, and the compas have dropped off a pile of hot tortillas for us. A good breakfast to start the day.

The heavy lifting for the water project starts today. Praxedis and I are going to oversee the strengthening of the spring box, while the compañeros begin digging the two kilometer trench to the distribution tank in the village. We will lay the pipes in the ditch, one 100-meter roll at a time, and connect them. The plan is to have water flowing through the pipe to the community in one week's time, but first we have to meet Maria at the riverbank. Hopefully she'll arrive safely, having travelled all night from San

Cristobal with the gear we need.

Sure enough, around 6 AM, we hear the sound of a pickup coming down the dirt track, pulling up on the opposite side of the river, honking away. Don Sisifo is already on that side of the river in the canoe awaiting the delivery.

The canoe is filled to capacity with the precious cargo but crosses safely, as always. Maria jumps out, full of joy. "We made it!"

She tells us that they left San Cristobal around midnight in a pickup driven by a local Zapatista compañero. Maria had curled up in the backseat as they passed through the valley's military checkpoint, and the driver had thrown a few blankets over her to disguise her petite form. The soldier manning the checkpoint—groggy at 4 AM—had only briefly scrutinized the vehicle and waved them through, uninterested in their cargo, which included the all-important picks and shovels for the project as well as more bags of cement, and other sundry plumbing bits and pieces.

His cargo unloaded, the compa in the pickup honks and turns the truck back towards San Cristobal... Mission accomplished.

With Maria back in the house, things start moving.

"Do you want to take a nap after the long night's journey?" I ask.

"No, fuck that, man. Let's get to work!"

Maria is a hard-working, no-nonsense gringa who hails from a long line of radicals. She ended up here via a deep commitment to social justice and direct action, most recently by supporting indigenous struggles at Black Mesa, and funded her activities by growing weed in her backyard. Technically proficient, she found herself participating in water projects as soon as she stepped foot in Chiapas, and even at a relatively tender age—her late twenties—she is most skilled water-operative in the zone. Naturally ambitious, her competitive streak often leads her to butt heads with other people working in the field. Type A personalities are generally in the minority in left solidarity milieus and are often viewed skeptically as "authoritarians" by other activists. Maria is the kind of person who accumulates associates more than she does friends or compañeros, but, nevertheless, she and I have become steadfast friends over the last couple of years. I admire her capacity to do, and trust her implicitly. Sometimes she can be bossy, but with her level of commitment, I can deal with that.

Maria calls a meeting with Don Sisifo and the water responsables, and together they hatch a plan. We work collectively, but
some personalities are more dynamic than others when it comes
to making things happen, and Maria is one of them. Maria pours
over charts and maps and works out the engineering of the project,
consulting Don Sisifo and showing him the plans, and people get
down to business.

Outsiders working in the zone often get carried away and think
they know it all. Academics would call it "the pathology of privilege"—where individuals from the US, Europe, or indeed, urban
metropolises like Mexico City, Buenos Aires, and Sao Paulo, think
they have all the answers, and think that people on the ground—
rustic indigenous, "backward" and uneducated—exist as mere re-
ceptors of their great knowledge.

We're aware of this pattern and try to deal with it as best we
can. Maria, as the brains of the operation, combats this pathology, or
paternalistic attitude, by prioritizing the perspective of the community, the grassroots, at all levels of decision making and learning. By
putting the indigenous voice and opinion first and then focusing on
the process, our progress might be slower or our efficiency less—as
we explain everything and involve the locals every step of the way—
but that's the nature of the work and goal. It's not just that the water
must be delivered, but that the people participate and become owners of their own system. They take control of their everyday life,
heighten the community's self-organization and strengthen their
ability to pursue their social, political, economic and cultural goals
and growth—this is autonomy. Revolution from the bottom up.

This kind of situated-learning methodology emphasizes
hands-on experience as crucial for real understanding. Praxedis,
who takes a keen interest in critical pedagogy, likes to quote Confucius: "Tell me, and I will forget. Show me, and I may remember.
Involve me, and I will understand."

"I didn't know that Confucius was an anarchist," says Maria,
chiding him.

"Everyone has an element of anarchy within them," replies
Praxedis. "Just they don't always know it. Even you Maria."

"I'm not sure about that at all, compa," laughs Maria. "I don't
think I'm cool enough to be an anarchist."

This is another thing about Maria. Despite being constantly

surrounded by them, she is a bit suspicious of anarchists. She recognizes that they are doing the heavy lifting in the movement in terms of organizing and direct action, but she has little truck with the more chaotic and destructive element of anarchy. I suspect that, as a bit of a control freak, she finds that sensibility somewhat threatening—it is, in a word, uncontrollable. ✗

The twenty-one compañeros have begun digging in earnest with the new tools, dividing the trench up into ten-meter sections. Each man works at his own pace using pick, shovel, and machetes to hack through roots. A couple of youngsters move up and down the ditch with heavy mallets breaking cumbersome rocks that impede the trench. As they zoom ahead, it's clear that these men can really work and they are highly motivated, but upon closer inspection, the trench seems too shallow in most places—only fifty centimeters when ideally it should be seventy. So we have to assume the overseer role, telling the toiling campesinos to dig deeper. We feel guilty—like we're bosses—this notion that we are "engineers" overseeing the operation while the others toil and labor digging through the rocks. It sucks.

I remember picking coffee alongside peasants in Nicaragua—people as poor as here in Roberto Arenas—and the mood was always boisterous and noisy. There was always salsa or some other form of raucous music blasting from battered tape recorders, and the sound of singing and laughing and shouting and arguing and playing around. Here everything is done more in silence than sound. Quietude abounds. Now, of course, digging a ditch is hardly easy-going work compared to picking coffee but here, no matter what the task, it is done very quietly. People talk their soft clicking language in hushed tones. The compas don't make any sound when they walk. The silence becomes surreal. It's like living in a waking dream populated by phantasmagorias, remote people who move fleetingly in and out of shadows and reflections. Not better, no worse, just different.

We dine in Doña Dolores's kitchen, enveloped, of course, in rich silence. The food is reduced to just the basics: beans and stale tortillas—and we reckon it's probably time to set up in our own kitchen and stop imposing on this kind family. A group of women and teenage girls are lingering around the doorway of the kitchen. We attempt to engage them—particularly Maria—but they are ferociously shy, and turn away giggling when addressed. Being the first caxlanes to work (or even visit) in this hamlet, we feel a pressure to break through this wall of wary distance, particularly among the women. So far they seem unsure of how to deal with us. Shy and withdrawn, they give us all the space in the world and appear to try to make us feel welcome without actually saying anything. They assume a most humble demeanour, besides the fact that few of them speak Spanish, rarely addressing us. As with the men, the women, too, use the common moniker "compa" hesitatingly, and sometimes completely disregard it for the more polite "Don" (or "Doña" for Maria). We feel uneasy using the familiar "tu" form when speaking with them, as if it might be perceived as patronizing instead of comradely.[1]

"Compañera," begins Doña Dolores, addressing Maria.

"Si, compañera?"

"The compañeras would like to invite you to visit the *hortaliza*

---

1. "Tu" is used informally between family and friends. Usted is the formal form of tu and is used to address figures of authority. Furthermore, if someone addresses you as 'usted' and you respond in "tu'"it can be perceived as patronizing.

[vegetable garden] with them tomorrow. They would like you to see their work and the food they are growing. Will you accept the invitation?"

"Of course! I would love to!"

Doña Dolores relates this news to the gaggle of young women lingering in the doorway.

"And can the compañeros, Praxedis and Ramon, come along too?" asks Maria.

Doña Dolores asks the women in Tzeltal.

"Yes, they say. They are welcome."

As they leave, each one comes in to the kitchen and delicately shakes our hands. Maria, Praxedis, and I are delighted. It is a big thrill to get invited to the hortaliza. The community is opening up to us!

We feel the quiet glow of incipient acceptance.

•••

I have begun to read Joseph Conrad's *Heart of Darkness* by candle-light. I didn't choose the book for any special reason—it just appeared as I left San Cristobal so I put it in my backpack. I didn't like it when I read it in college, years ago, and I don't like it now, but it is quite an apt book for this jaunt. Not so much for the jungle location, nor the white man's experience in alien cultures, and the reminder of a brutal colonialist past—although these are useful subjects to dwell on—but for the comparison between the torment these early capitalist adventurers suffered in Congo at the hands of the locals, compared to the rich, enveloping welcome we receive from our hosts. Of course, while we may be the first outsiders/foreigners ever to step foot in this hamlet we are not extracting mineral wealth, enslaving the locals or whipping them to work harder, but volunteer comrades who support their revolt and are working with them. Some would say that, as activists, we are extracting something more precious than all the coveted metals in the world: hope. It's something to take back with us to our homelands and our own political struggles, but I think that is a cynical take. Anyhow, who is going home? Where is home? We are here to stay, throwing our lot in with the Zapatistas, and even if we are extracting hope, dreams, metaphysical wealth, in receiving we are doing our best to give back as well.

It is a fine thing to read *Heart of Darkness* critically, as a lived-experience rather than a literary text to study. So while Conrad may be attempting to portray the Heart of Darkness as the white man's soul's descent into horror in the bleakness of darkest Africa, we subscribe more to the political critique of Chinua Achebe. That Nigerian author sees Conrad's book more useful as a study of the despicable nature of raw capitalist exploitation and the ideology of imperialism that renders Africa "a place of negations," devoid of history, culture, and language. Worse still, Africa and its people serve as a mere backdrop for Conrad, in which he explores the mental disintegration of one rogue imperialist. As usual, it is all about whitey.

"Can nobody see the preposterous and perverse arrogance," writes Achebe, "in thus reducing Africa to the role of props for the break-up of one petty European mind?"

The heart of darkness, the "horror, the horror" that Conrad discovers, is not the Congo jungle environment, nor the savage, cannibal natives, but the morally repugnant nature of the white colonizer's endeavours there within.

Of course, we as solidarity activists place ourselves more in the tradition of another whitey, the Irish revolutionary Roger Casement, who famously exposed the barbarity of the European-operated rubber trade in Congo in his Casement Report of 1904, and subsequently organized a successful worldwide campaign against such brutal capitalist exploitation. Casement was initially positioned in the Congo as a British consul, but in an early harbinger for international solidarity practice, he turned his position of privilege into a weapon for justice against the marauding imperialism.

Conrad and Casement were in the Congo at the same time and serve as interesting contrasts, showing how two people can look upon the same situation from different perspectives. Where Conrad saw the horror of a white man's mind disintegrating, Casement saw the horror of a culture and people being decimated.

So *Heart of Darkness* is a fitting book to accompany the work, lots of food for thought as we spend the next few days laying the lines and digging the trench. Carrying heavy and bulky 1 inch rolls of plastic pipe to the point where the water flows from the last pipe, we stagger past the men toiling in the trench and hook the pipes up to the line. Then we busy ourselves with more technical details, figuring out pressure and head and mapping the territory. And I wonder what the compañeros are thinking of us? Maria,

Praxedis, and I, dilettantes fiddling with the pipes while they do the heavy lifting and digging? Because we are "engineers"—ahem, intellectual workers—we are exempt from the hard labor?

"Time to join the compas at the coalface," Praxedis suggests, and Maria and I are on board.

Putting aside the pipes and our "engineer" caps, we pick up hoes and get working with the compañeros on the trench. After the initial mirth—men put down their tools just to watch the caxlanes digging the ditch, particularly a woman caxlan!—our proximity and shared endeavour ultimately allows for a new intimacy.

"The men are impressed that you can dig," Vicente, the water responsable tells us.

"We thought rich people couldn't do hard labor like us indigenous."

Which is ironic, of course—we can dig and have done so throughout our lives. Will I tell him how I worked on various construction sites across Europe since I was a teenager? Or that Maria was a gardener and carpenter, and Praxedis has done every kind of physical labor imaginable in Mexico City and beyond? Neither are we rich! But it is all relative. I suppose we aren't condemned to a life of eternal labor without remittance. Their toiling Sisyphus to our fanciful Jason searching for golden fleeces.[2]

But soon such cerebral meanderings are superseded by the discomfort and pain of the hard, monotonous digging. Hands are covered in fresh blisters, muscles ache, backs are sore, and the sun beats down unmercifully. The soil is hard and stony, and teeming with life: worms, insects, and various strange and tiny creatures. Soon my hands and arms are coated with sticky mud, and flies loiter irritatingly around my sweaty head. And then, with sudden intensity, a tropical rain shower drenches us and everything else for ten dramatic minutes, and just as abruptly, the sun reappears and we are dry and parched again. And when we rest on our picks and shovels, conversations strike up. Other compas join in a discussion with Maria, Praxedis, and me about the *Heart of Darkness*. We give a brief outline of the plot and the events of the book. The compas are not terribly shocked about the conditions

2. Jason was an ancient Greek mythological hero, famous as the leader of the Argonauts who wandered the oceans in their quest for a golden-haired winged ram—the mythical golden fleece.

in Congo—a place none have heard of—or the gruesome pun-
ishments such as cutting off the hands of unproductive, rubber-
extracting native workers.

"Such things occurred on the *fincas* [plantations] in the time of
our fathers and grandfathers," says Gordo.

"Or worse," says Alfredo.

"Much worse," says Vicente.

"In the time of our great-grandfathers such things happened
all the time," Gordo says, authoritatively.

"The indigenous who slaved long hours logging the great trees
by hand for the big companies, were beaten and flogged, hung alive
from trees and left for days and nights in the jungle."

Ah yes, the infamous mahogany industry of Chiapas in the
early 1900s as documented by the other book I am reading at the
moment, B. Traven's *Rebellion of the Hanged*. Traven describes
scenes to match the worst of the Congo excesses as the mahogany
cutters on the *monteria* (labor camps) rebel against their intolerable
conditions and start a local revolution.

Traven, a mysterious German anarchist who fled Europe after
the failed Bavarian Soviet uprising in Munich, 1919, wound up in
Chiapas, and reputedly lived for several years amongst indigenous
Tsotsils in the isolated highlands. His six famous books, which
are set in this region—"the Jungle Novels"—are an interesting literary contrast to *Heart of Darkness*. Traven turns the all-pervasive
"whitey in exotic lands" perspective—a narrative I'm sure you,
dear reader, are quite getting bored with by now—on its head.
Narrated from the indigenous perspective instead of the colonialists, it ends with insurrection, rather than capitulation. Though
in contrast to Roger Casement, the clandestine Traven didn't
engage in any kind of solidarity with the wretched of the earth
whom he found himself among, nor did he start a campaign, or
join a revolution—he merely wrote stories about what he saw and
heard and imagined.

"One becomes a philosopher," wrote Traven, "by living
among people who are not of his own race and who speak a different language ... A trip to a Central American jungle to watch
how Indians behave near a bridge won't make you see either the
jungle or the bridge or the Indians if you believe that the civilization you were born into is the only one that counts. Go and look

around with the idea that everything you learned in school and college is wrong."[3]

"Hideous Indian Women"

Dawn outside. Light creeps slowly into this mountain-framed valley. Horses move around outside in the grass, pigs and chickens loiter. It's 6 AM.

"Wake up, imperialists!" says Praxedis—already doing push-ups outside the doorway. He mocks Maria and me for being quasi-imperialists because we have brought mosquito nets to cover our bare board beds. And we have sleeping bags. How indulgent!

Today has the makings of an exciting day because we have a date to visit the ladies in their vegetable garden! Accordingly, it means we are only working a half day in the trench, because the limited supply of hoes is needed for the hortaliza. My whole body sighs in relief.

Our field kitchen is very basic—a wood fire upon an earthen table—and we emerge to find Praxedis has kindly prepared eggs and an ocean of coffee. Our food supplies are tied from the roof in bags because the rats are having midnight feasts of whatever is left on our lone shelf. There are ants everywhere. Nevertheless, it feels homey and we are content here. Garbed in our now-muddy, ripped, and well-worn working clothes; heavy boots caked in mud; machetes by our sides, we set off. Every day we resemble the compas more, except that their clothes and boots, despite being well worn, are always immaculately clean and fresh every morning. The men's wives—the clothes washers—are doing a great job.

The men are already up in the trench, digging away. By mid-morning, the temperature will soar above 40 degrees Celsius. Even they look completely knackered by working in this heat—some look close to heat exhaustion. Each has their quota of ten meters a day, and on scorching days like this, it must feel like ten kilometers.

---

3. Traven. B. 1966. *The Bridge in the Jungle*. New York: Alfred A Knopf p. 23.

We notice some men are only going down thirty centimeters on the rocks, which is not good enough—must dig deeper!—but to not to sap morale on this challenging day, we decide not to say anything. We can come back to it later.

Meanwhile, we three caxlanes are too parched to dig a second longer, and, recognizing our own personal limits, busy ourselves preparing rolls of pipe and coupling connections. It's time to hook up another three rolls of pipe—300 meters more in total.

A group of compañeros unroll the pipe by hoisting the heavy tubing on a pole and unwinding it awkwardly. If it gets kinked, the tubing cracks, rendering it useless, so this job has got to be done right. It is slow, tricky work.

The tubes are laid out in the trench, but now connecting the pipes is proving difficult. We need to insert short plastic couplings between the two pipe-ends, and the problem is that it's always a tight fit, and the connection needs to be made with force. And the whole exercise is complicated further because water is flowing out of one of the pipes with plentiful force. Time and time again we heat the hard PVC with the highly flammable oil resin *ocote*, then push and huff and puff and pull and get wet and fall over and the coupling just won't fucking go in! Not enough lubrication! Once more, and somewhat comically, Praxedis and I face each other, heat up the pipes, and thrust down, pushing with all our might, grunting and gasping. The spectacle brings more compas around to watch the show. They laugh and whistle and act as if it is the funniest thing ever. Eventually, kid gloves off, we both exercise maximum force—strained muscles, Neanderthal screams, and it finally slides in. It's still half an inch shy of being flush but fuck it, we say, let's put on double braces to secure. I had indeed forgotten the joys of putting that stuff together.

Now the line is 500 meters long, but the water is gulping out in spurts, suggesting an air-bubble further up the line. So we fiddle about with the reservoir tank at the spring, securing the globe-valve even more tightly, trying not to interrupt the flow of water. This constant revision and tinkering is time consuming but obligatory—it's what "engineers" do.

It's time to visit the hortaliza. The patch is located a little beyond the community, down a small valley beside the river—a pretty location with easy access to water. About fifteen women are gathered there, many with babies on their backs, *rebozo* style,[4] and lots of very small kids are playing at the edge of the patch. Each woman wears the traditional dress, a blaze of lurid primary colors, and each has a machete or hoe in hand. They greet us cheerfully, and half of them, the younger ones, are giggling uncontrollably, at what exactly, I don't know, but it is amusing to see. So we are all off to a smiley start.

The vegetable patch is roughly a square half-acre of well-worked soil in raised beds, enclosed by a chicken wire fence. In one luxuriant corner a blaze of green vegetables are beginning to spout.

"The women's collective began the hortaliza earlier this year, after we attended a workshop in the caracol," explains Doña Dolores, who seems to act as the spokesperson for the rest, and whose command of Spanish is greater than she had been initially letting on. She is referring to the regular hortaliza workshops in the Zapatista center at La Garrucha. "The compañeras learned how to improve the diet of the children, to give them more vitamins."

---

4. Slung over the shoulder in a woven blanket.

Were there vegetables in the community before?

"A little," replied Doña Dolores. "Just what people grew in their backyard. But this hortaliza produces plenty for every family."

With a tap on location—as is planned with the water project—it will be easier to water the hortaliza and will be more efficient.

We are shown around the budding rows of cabbage, celery, onions, tomatoes, and radish, all grown without chemical fertilizer—it is organic. The soil in the raised beds is loamy and well drained. The women have begun turning over the soil to begin another larger growing patch. They received a batch of new seeds at the caracol, and are planting today. These women are no strangers to agricultural work of course. Apart from kitchen work, raising children, tending to livestock in the yard, they also work in the family corn-patch, whether planting, weeding, or harvesting. So the hortaliza is one more responsibility on top of an already busy schedule.

And yet, everyone is cheery and excited by the tasks at hand. What is noticeable is the unity of purpose in their manner of working. They line up and work together at the same pace, side by side, raking the earth, and moving in cohesion, almost as one. It seems a very natural, collective way of working.

If solidarity is unity of purpose or togetherness, then these women have perfected it. But it's not just solidarity; it is something else. Nobody told everyone to get in line and work in tandem, they just moved instinctively into place and form a single, non-separated body. This kind of cohesion is born in community, of people living in each other's shadows. This isn't solidarity—not even reciprocity—it is more an intrinsic form of community harmony.

And so the afternoon evolves and we all lend a hand—raking, weeding, planting—busy as bees. The compañeras are so good-humored, and despite language difficulties, laughter blossoms between us. At the finish, a young compañera, Adelita, invites us to her house to eat.

She is a gregarious twenty-something-year-old woman with an easy silver-toothed smile, who, having overcome her initial shyness with us, reveals a good command of Spanish. She and Maria are getting on famously.

Adelita's house is typical for Roberto Arenas: wooden

structure, earthen floor, and sheet metal roofing, but it is warm and welcoming, and the cooking fire in the corner is like a hearth. She lives with her mother, brother, and her two children. We ask about her husband, and she replies only "He is gone," not revealing whether he left or died.

Sunlight flickers through the cracks in the wall and the beams of light dance around the smoke from the fire that Doña Consuela, Adelita's elderly mother, tends. It's a sumptuous rustic vision that disguises the deadly effects of the open fire—it causes so many pulmonary ailments for the kitchen workers—predominantly in the women of the house.

We are served beans on freshly made corn tortillas. It is a delicious treat. The rest of the family lingers in the background and, breaking protocol a little, we insist that they join us at the table.

We don't really talk much, just compliment the food, laugh with the children, and ask a few questions, which Adelita translates for her mother. The family came from a community further up the valley and we learn that Doña Consuela has never been to "the city"—Ocosingo—having spent her whole life in the forest and mountains. Adelita has been to the city and that is why she has a little Spanish. She explains that she brought her little five-year-old daughter there for medical attention. The gorgeous little girl, named Marisol, smiles widely as she hears her mother mentioning her name. "Marisol was very sick, and we had to take her to the nearest hospital in Ocosingo. She almost died. But, thank God, now she is almost better."

"What was wrong with her?"

"Measles," she explains. "With diarrhea and pneumonia."

We all look at this smiling, shining orb of a child, and thank God too.

Maria hugs her.

As the night begins to envelop us, we sit in comfortable silence around a single candle. There is only the sound of the crackling log fire in the corner and the flickering shadows from the soft flame dancing on the rough wooden walls as we journey towards night.

And then, all of a sudden, Adelita begins to sing; the lone voice in the semi-darkness. She sings a sad lilting lament like an old Irish *sean-nós* and the words go something like this:

How sad it is for the people
Who live in the communities
Suffering oppression
On top of illnesses and disease.
And to make things even worse
The army comes in
To terrorize the people
And steal their land away.
And we see the poor women
Forced into prostitution.
So with this final verse
Compañeras in the struggle
That you find encouragement from this song
And that God will hear our call.

Her tender singing trails off into the ether, along with the smoke from the fire. And so we return to silence again, but this time, the space filled with the haunting lyrics of Adelita's song.

"It is a song I learned when I was in the mountains with the compañeras, the Zapatista women," she says quietly.

As we leave, we shake hands with everyone, and Doña Consuela speaks to us directly and quite earnestly in Tzeltal. She gives each of us a fleeting embrace.

"My mother thanks you for coming here and helping the poor people. May God bless you," Adelita says.

It is a very touching moment. We are all a little speechless and, feeling very humbled, we stumble out of the smoky hut into the quiet night. The dark sky over the valley is starry and vast, and induces a feeling of infinite melancholy.

Later, snug under my imperialist mosquito netting, I read by flickering candlelight, but colonial literature like *Heart of Darkness* induces a feeling of nausea. I keep thinking of a passage of English author Graham Greene's 1938 book, *The Lawless Roads*, in which he describes his travels, by foot, in Chiapas. He wasn't fond of the place, as is his prerogative: "I loathed Mexico" he wrote, lamenting that there was "no escape from this country that I hated."[5] So it goes, some visitors like Mexico, some don't.

But then there is the despicable passage where he finds himself

---

5. Green, Graham. 1971. *The Lawless Roads*. New York: Penguin Books p. 184.

in an indigenous rural home in the Chiapas jungle, mu[ ] one we had just visited, and writes:

> Out from an inner room...came a little party of Indian women, tiny and bowed, old and hideous at 20. With their cave-dwellers' faces, and their long staffs they might have been Stone Age people emerging from forgotten caverns to pay their tribute to the redeemer on resurrection morning.[6]

Apologists dismiss this kind of callous xenophobia as a case of Greene merely being a "man of his time." But this is not acceptable: he reduces the indigenous to a grotesque caricature, conveying a notion of inferiority. It is racist, imperialist, and unforgivable. I think of Doña Consuelo, Adelita, Marisol, and the humble dwelling I have just departed. The sadness I feel for the deep-rooted injustice all around me gives way to an anger that finds expression in my clenched fist.

Digging with Conrad

And the next day we lose Maria. While Praxedis and I sleep soundly—as is wont in the jungle—accompanied by a rich, evocative dreamscape, poor Maria spent the night running for the nearby bushes, emptying her entire insides again and again, the victim of some foreign agent. It doesn't matter how long one spends in the communities, one is always liable to fall prey to a vicious tummy bug. Shit happens. We all know what it is like, this spontaneous evacuation of the entire contents of one's bowels; we all hate it, fear it, and can't avoid it. The horror, the horror. So Maria has been vomiting and shitting all night along, and now she is lying on her bed—pale, groaning softly—and there is nothing to be done. "I can't move," she says. Don't worry, stay there, we'll bring you water, it will pass.

---

6. Ibid., p.190.

There is no point giving her anything to eat. Everything will come up or out immediately. Water with a little salt will be the sum total of her input today.

Praxedis and I leave her to rest and we head to work. We bump into a gaggle of children, who ask, "Where's Maria?"

"In bed, sick."

And they rush off to see their favorite gringa. No rest for the weary, but at least she will have company.

And then there were two. We, the water team, are having a disastrous week, health-wise: I sliced my hand with a machete while cutting wood for the kitchen fire, adding to my two festering blisters from working the pick. I wrap my wounded mitt in bandages and tie it in my old Zapatista paliacate, rendering the scarf less ornate than when I sport it, revolutionary chic, around my neck. The same day, Praxedis slipped in the watery ditch, twisting his ankle and almost putting his back out. We have to laugh at ourselves; we resemble a mini-disaster zone for petty ailments. At least my trench foot from the journey over the mountains is getting better now. I come across more debonair when not limping like Quasimodo.

Despite the battlefield conditions today, we advance.

And now, it's porter time! Not the Guinness, but the one-inch pipes. One hundred meters of it—thirty kilos worth to be portered over one kilometer. We are connecting more sections of pipe and getting soaked in the process. What does it matter though, when there is a sudden and instant downpour—a flash flood, as such? The heavens open and a deluge is unleashed; an astonishing exhibition of the sublime power of nature. We smile disconsolate and continue the slog, wet to the bone, and splashing about in pools of rain that have filled the trench, and it is comically absurd.

Soon we're connecting the pipes again with glee. When they slide in as they should we are elated, and when it's not happening, we're incessantly frustrated. Today the work flows well, and Vicente smiles at us. We smile back; a smile of complicity, of fraternity, not a mask of a smile. Other compas still treat us referentially or as objects of bizarre interest. They laugh at our antics, but not with us. It's an important breakthrough, Vicente and Gordo and a few others are smiling *with* us. Midday, we make our way home in the mud, covered head to toe, soaked, but content that we did three rolls today and water now flows steadily out of the pipes at 900 meters—almost half-way there. The compas are encouraged to see it functioning.

In the afternoon, Praxedis and I join the men in the trench to dig, and as usual I fuck myself up, gouging out a piece of my palm with the pick. Adding that to the wickerwork of cuts, blisters, and sores, I have a proper medical case in my hands alone. Today I'm feeling the dying. My limbs are sore, covered in cuts and blisters, aches and pains everywhere.

"This labor is hard on the body. Are you suffering, Ramon?" asks Gordo sympathetically.

He gets an earful of grumbles and complaints. I show him my mangled hands.

But nothing compares to putting things in perspective. Gordo begins to wax lyrical about various accidents and injuries sustained by people here in the community. Like the compa who chopped his thumb off with a machete, the kid who fell into the river and almost drowned, and—the most chilling—the compa Alberto, who poked himself in the eye with a stick as he dug a hole and lost the eye, because it took him a day to get himself to the nearest clinic.

At the state hospital in Ocosingo, they decided to remove the injured eye rather than treat it, cheaper probably. There he is, the same Alberto who accompanied us over the mountains, still wandering around with a paliacate tied around his head. I had assumed he had a temporary infection or something, but the notion that he has that neckerchief tied over his missing eye for the rest of his life is deeply disturbing.

OK. That puts me in place; I shut up about my minor woes.

Returning to the schoolhouse in the afternoon, we are greeted by the cutest sight: little Marisol, Adelita's daughter, is sitting by the edge of Maria's bed as she sleeps. The child is watching over her through her illness.

"Marisol, you are an angel."

I search around my backpack and find my emergency chocolate bar ("break open only in dire need"). In an act that I don't regret to admit was not easy for me, I present it to the child.

"Thank you for taking care of Maria while she is sick, Marisol."

The little girl smiles and hides it in her blouse. In another infinitely endearing act, we hear later that, instead of enjoying the chocolate bar herself, she in turn presented it to her mother.

Praxedis is proving to be something of a prince. He cooks up some lovely rice and beans, and a couple of kids drop off some hot tortillas in a pretty napkin—fine delicious tortillas, handmade of corn grown in the milpas just on the other side of the hill. Absolutely scrumptious. Don Sisifo drops in to the kitchen. He is upbeat and happy with the progress.

"The compas are very content," he tells us. "It is all good."

He lingers a few seconds in the doorway. Will he actually chill out, stay for a moment, and chat for the first time ever? No, he quickly excuses himself after informing us that he has some fences to mend. Well built, sturdy and muscular, he is a relentless work machine. When carrying cement or whatever on his back, mecapal style, he assumes the gait of a sturdy shire horse. Although a comparison to a Greek god would be more appropriate than a shire horse, the metaphor remains constant: Don Sisifo, the man who never, ever stops laboring.

Like this new day, which, like the day before, brings more toil: hours and hours of digging under the hot sun. Don Sisifo leads by example, and he is the first to carry the plastic rolls, clambering up and down gullies, over boulders, along the rough riverbank, acting like it's a stroll in the park—as if work absolves the body, sweats out impurities. Prompted by his lead, the compas dig faster. This particular section of the dig, in the river basin, is through pure soil. With no roots or rocks, things move more swiftly. Everyone is quite happy. The sun is shining majestically and Praxedis and I have got the joining of the tubes down pat. He does the pushing and I am the anchor. It works. It's almost there. Fast work.

"Praxedis!" exclaims Gordo, as he comes up the line. "There's a bit of a leak in the pipe!"

I spoke too soon.

Alarm Bells!

Praxedis and I rush to the emergency spot, and find that there are two small holes in the pipe at about the 1,000 meter point. It's moles! A certain mountain variety who have developed a taste for plastic pipe. It has all gone too smoothly until now and no project is ever without its formidable difficulties. However, seepage from the little gnawed holes is derisory. We apply some tape and *voila!*, it's fixed—but the resident moles could present difficulties later on.

Back at base, two days into her intense tummy bug, Maria still alternates between chills and fever, not seeming to be getting better. The kids' constant attention hasn't had physical benefits and she is still feeling pretty wretched.

Don't worry, I tell her, give it a couple of days, you will be fine.

"Fuck this shit, dude. I'm thinking I might cut out. I'm completely exhausted, and I can't fucking work if I'm pissing out my ass every ten minutes."

I reckon another factor is that she probably just doesn't want to be a non-productive entity, a burden on the water project and the community. We have only a few more days of fairly straightforward digging work ahead of us here, so her presence won't be that necessary. What's more, there is plenty of preparation to be done, back in San Cristobal, for the next phase.

We have a group of five volunteers coming to participate in the final stage of the water project: constructing the distribution tank and distribution lines within the community. These newcomers need to be introduced to the project and prepped. Maria could well occupy her time with them, as well as do accounts and get supplies for the next stage. And then there is the international donor, solidarity, and NGO sector to follow up on. Seeing as the estimate for this water project is in the region of $6,000 for materials and transport alone, Maria needs to get on top of all that stuff, the "industry" side of solidarity business.

We call a meeting with Don Sisifo and the water responsables, and ask Adelita and another compañera from the hortaliza to come along too. Maria wants to help the women and knows that things will only happen if the agreement is made at a group meeting. Other compañeros join the meeting—like the Galician fishermen look-alikes, for no other reason than because they want to. Add the gaggle of children and we now have a good twenty people in the schoolroom. Maria, visibly shaking with globs of sweat matting her brow, outlines the next stage of the work.

We draw up a plan for Maria's absence and reflect on the work already done.

There is a moment of tension when Maria asks Adelita a question about the hortaliza, and Don Sisifo answers.

"I am wondering what the compañera thinks of this," asserts Maria.

But Adelita only says quietly, "As Don Sisifo said..."

An uncomfortable silence.

Maria leaves in the middle of the night, dragging herself out of the schoolroom, and heads to the riverbank, where Don Sisifo waits to row her across to catch the only bus to town, which passes around 4 AM. A dingy, rust-bucket of a chicken bus picks Maria up for the journey back to San Cristobal. It's remarkable that it can make it through the rough mountain path.

Praxedis and I are taking the reins. There is a ton of work to be done but we are confident that we can get it all done in a week. We need to finish the trench, lay the rest of the pipes, and prepare a concrete base for the distribution tank.

The days pass by, punctuated by digging, digging, and more digging. Like a chain gang, we take our positions in the trench each morning, mark out ten meters and begin our day's labor. One grips the pick and its dirt-encrusted wooden stalk receives dirt-encrusted hands; like a hand in a glove they become one, body and tool merging. The first crunch as the metal thuds into the hard earth resounds throughout one's entire body, and then the body resigns itself to a long day of heavy laboring, begrudgingly accepting its role. It is only later in the day, when the muscles are worn and the mind gets weary that the body starts refusing. But in between, when your body is dealing, your mind can rise above, thoughts flourishing. Sometimes one dwells on the immediate job at hand and the rocks and the stones, the method, sometimes one thinks of people and times, melancholy or nostalgic. Occasionally the mind soars, and digging becomes a transcendental joy. Those moments, however, are rare. Usually one is more preoccupied with blisters and mire.

Drained from toiling under the burning sun, Praxedis and I climb out of the ditch and begin the more leisurely task of casing out the location for the village's distribution tank. We have chosen a spot on protected, high, flat ground. We need to completely level the area where the tank will sit. Sharing a single pick we work the earth and clear a patch for the tank, grading a spot seven meters squared. We stop for matz and a smoke and enjoy what feels like the first rest in days—and well deserved it is, too. Could it be the first break in eleven days? Campo life: it's all physical.

But, soon enough, we're back at it again. The site has to be perfectly level, because a 13,000 liter concrete water tank will be sitting on top of it. It is tedious work, done mostly on our hands and knees, taking approximations with the levelling tool. We attached the short level to a long pipe and that suffices. We mark out a circle, flatten it down, and level it again. Like nineteenth-century work, but it gets done: appropriate technology and us covered in mud.

Then we take another long break and tramp off up the trench with another roll, the two-and-a-half inch size rolls are too heavy for one, so we carry it between us on a pole. The compas digging have reached the two-thirds mark! That was quick! Are they digging deep enough? I would say yes, more or less. We can go back later and revise the shallow spots. This constant worry that the trench not deep enough is an albatross on the shoulders of us conscientious engineers.

By now, the compas are digging along the banks of the river—treacherous, rocky terrain filled with trees, roots blocking the trench's trail. Despite constant hacking at the roots, the workers can only get down about thirty centimeters. The digging is haphazard, slow, and awkward, and there is the added problem of potential flooding here if the river breaks its banks, which would wash away the pipes. Praxedis and I wander up and down this section with a couple of heavy sledgehammers, smashing rocks that block the line. It is mind-numbing and brutal work, whacking at heavy boulders, the thumps shuddering the core of our beings. Can't take too much of that without inducing a lobotomy, so off we go to the more leisurely activity of connecting lines of pipe. By the end of the day, we have connected three 100-meter rolls—that's 1,300 meters done. There's no more engineering work to oversee, and no other reason to not return to the trench, so like two condemned men we pick up a couple of sledgehammers, and join the men, knee deep in the ditch.

There is always one thing to look forward to at the end of every day's labor—apart from it being over at long last—and that is our pilgrimage to the river. The men split to their various houses and do whatever they do after work. Lie around in a hammock? Play with their kids? Make out with their wives? I don't know, but they always disappear for a couple of hours, leaving the village deserted. (With the exception of Don Sisifo who I'm sure uses this in-between time to mend fences or something.) So the caxlanes relocate to the decadent and stunningly gorgeous riverside beach for our daily bathing indulgence. "Zapatista Springs," we name the location in honor of those cynics who deem Chiapas little more than a vacation spot for revolutionary tourists.

To bathe in the now-clear and sparkling Jataté at the end of the day is one of our simple pleasures. The lush water washes over our weary, mud-encrusted bodies like a balm. Gorgeous nature. We bathe and wash, swim, or clean our clothes or we just sit about reading and relaxing, knowing the joy of lazy late afternoons in the bosom of this Lacandon Jungle bower, when the sun no longer burns, only caresses.

Everyday we are joined at this lonely and secluded stretch of river, a little upstream from the community, by a teenager who smiles a timid *buenas tardes*, and never says a word more. Today, around 5 PM we hear the familiar rustling of the trees and the patter of flip-flops on the forest path as the young girl arrives. She sets up camp about ten meters further up and begins her routine of washing her long black hair and some pieces of clothing. At first we wonder why she chooses to come here; all the other women go to the specially designated women-only spot along the riverbank to wash, and if she doesn't like it there, there are numerous other coves and inlets along this stretch where she can do her routine. But it is pleasant to have her silent company. We caxlanes like this spot because there is a little stretch of sand giving it a beachy feel, as well as a feeling of seclusion, since it's off the beaten track a little. Other spots are shared with horses, pigs, and other livestock, but not here. Maybe we are a little squeamish about who we share our bathing water with. Perhaps she is too...

Unfailingly, this young girl smiles beguilingly at Praxedis, strips off her top, and begins soaping her beautiful, shining hair, then her arms and body. The routine lasts for ten minutes and she becomes completely absorbed in the task, as if oblivious to the rest of the world, and to him.

"Your admirer's beauty ritual," I comment, teasing Praxedis. He is highly embarrassed by the girl's apparent infatuation with him, and expresses his chagrin by pretending that it is not happening and that she's actually not there. But when he strips off his shirt, revealing his toned, tattooed torso, he is fully aware that the girl's gaze is devouring his flesh. With a body like his who wouldn't be a proud exhibitionist seeking out an audience? And, with this smitten youngster, he has a loyal devotee.

This day, a canoe comes passing by: Don Sisifo is on his way to go fishing. He sees us and waves, and then with a skilled ferryman's finesse, directs the small craft over to the bank.

Good afternoon, he says, pleasantly.

"Good afternoon Don Sisifo. How are you?"

Going up river, he tells us, pointing that way.

"To fish."

Really?

"In order to feed my family."

Maybe he said that to assure us that he isn't skiving off to do some leisurely angling, or a spot of bird-spotting. No, he's working. Still. OK, we got that and now we feel even more decadent and depraved lying around in our underwear on this sandy beach with his petulant teenage daughter just a stones throw away, similarly half naked and indolent.

"That is my daughter," he says, ignoring her. "Her name is Dolores, like her mother."

That must be confusing in the house!

"No. I call her '*hija*' — daughter."

Don Sisifo has eight children by his account, and nine according to Doña Dolores. We deduce that she's counting one of her eldest daughter's children, whom she's raising.

Sisifo changes the subject.

"She likes you, compañero," he says, addressing Praxedis. "Do you have a wife?"

"No!" says Praxedis, spluttering.

"My daughter would make a good wife. She is a hard worker." He smiles. I think he is being deadly serious. Praxedis is flapping around nervously like a monk in a brothel.

"She is ready for a husband," he says. "If you married her we will give you a milpa, and a plot to put your house."

"Eh, you are fortunate to have such a pretty daughter," says Praxedis, "but she is very young, far too young for me."

"She is fifteen now. Here the girls marry at this age."

And its true, here in the communities, it is often the case that as soon as the girl is biologically ready, she is carted off to be married and procreate. In other communities, women are fighting back against that custom, but maybe not so much here. Joining the EZLN, the Zapatista Army, provides another means of escaping early marriage. But we haven't met any women combatants in this community.

"You can have her for a crate of soda and a couple of chickens."

Don Sisifo has entered into the business of dowry making without much ado.

"No, Don Sisifo. No, thank you," says Praxedis with some finality, mortified.

The next day we return to the usual riverside spot and, sure enough, along comes young Dolores. Praxedis greets her, somewhat embarrassedly, but she very distinctly looks the other way—as if it was some kind of imposition, or as if he doesn't exist. The heartbreaking news has clearly been passed on by Don Sisifo—that Praxedis didn't take him up on the offer of her hand in marriage. Was the price of a crate of soda and a couple of chickens too much? Or too little? It seems to me that Don Sisifo offered a well-below-market-price for the girl because both he and she were keen for the deal to go through. Alas, too keen.

Today, she languidly soaps up her hair, washes her body, and acts like a movie star entrenched in a tragic role. Praxedis gets on with his washing ritual more stiffly and rigid than usual. I stay in the background, scribbling notes (these notes) and snickering at them both.

•••

Back at base, the children march around chanting with greater excitement, sensing the adults' growing anticipation of the arriving water. The children's young voices are shrill and enchanting: "*Zapata vive, la lucha sigue*," "*El pueblo unido, jamas sera vencido*," etc.[7]

Our kitchen is good, we eat well, though perhaps a little basic. No dairy, meat, wheat, or anything sweet. Just tortillas, rice, beans, spuds, garlic, onions, and salsa. Complete overhaul of my diet! At least there is plenty of coffee. Tonight, Praxedis cooks up some yummy, spicy-bean tacos in home-made tortillas—someday he will make someone a very happy spouse. Over sacred coffee, we talk of other places: of Brazil, of Greece, of Praxedis's travels, of my trav-

---

7. "Zapata lives, the struggle continues." "The people united will never be defeated." Two ubiquitous chants at any Zapatista manifestation.

els, of other worlds, of the globe, our love of the sea, of the road, of moving, of exploring, the usual.

How did Praxedis arrive here, digging ditches in Planet Lacandon?

Destiny or default, he is not sure, but he grew up a rebel in Mexico City. From a tender age, Praxedis was involved in the radical milieu that has a long and profound history of flourishing in the great and monstrous metropolis. Anarchism attracted him for its spirit of emancipation and practical application, and he, like a few other of his fellow city activist-kind, heard the Zapatista clarion call and came down to join in. As an urban worker whose skills were not so necessary in the rural makeup of the battlefront, finding the right role was difficult for him. He put his hand to jungle life for a while, before the Zapatista command stepped in and requested that he and his ilk of urban radicals employ their talents in other fields. "We have plenty of local volunteers here, go foment revolution in other places," they ordered. So he went back to Mexico City, tried for a while to "foment revolution," but felt crushed by the Sisyphean task in such a giant urban space. He drove a taxi, travelled a bit, read theory and philosophy, and then realized

he yearned for the Zapatista environment. And so he returned, getting involved in water projects.

Was it the right thing to do?

"For me, yeah. I wasn't getting anything done in Mexico City. The city was sucking my soul dry."

It is true, he does thrive in the rural setting.

So are you here for the long term then?

"Yeah. I'm only going back to Mexico City at the head of a long rebel column taking over the Capital!"

But , I intervene—playing devil's advocate—first of all, the Zapatistas are not anarchist, and secondly, I very much doubt that taking over Mexico City in a long rebel column is part of the program.

"Yeah," he laughs. "I'm projecting."

"So what are you doing here with this 'armed reformist outfit?'" I pose, using a term hard-left detractors often ply.

"Look, we know the Zapatistas, in the here and now, are not some revolutionary ideal. Yeah we know the EZLN it is a top-down, authoritarian, paternalistic organization, and we are fully aware that the majority of the base is devoutly religious, superstitious, nationalistic and socially conservative."

I'm on my way out the door to start packing my backpack.

"But, he continues, what we do have is a radical anti-state and anti-capitalist movement, and they are organized and resisting. There is nothing like them in the whole of Mexico, or indeed anywhere. And they are in movement, moving towards a better future. Reality and politics are in flux, and the Zapatistas are still in the becoming stage. They are addressing their internal problems like authoritarianism and patriarchy, and they are confronting the external ones, like taking a clear anti-capitalist line. The Zapatistas are going in the right direction; they are vibrant and I'm here to push it a little more in an anarchistic direction if I can. But I don't mean just me—me as a part of a collective effort: all the other caxlan compañeros here. We are all in this together."

OK, unpack the bags, the revolution is still on course.

"So what do you think is the basis of the relationship between anarchism and Zapatismo? Why are all the anarchists so excited about the Zapatistas?" I ask.

"Anarchists and Zapatistas are not one and the same," continues Praxedis. "We are fellow travellers, at best. Anarchists are attracted to the organizational model of the Zapatistas: community-based participatory democracy and the demand for autonomy. We admire their militant resistance to neo-liberalism. We share their anti-capitalist stance. But our support for the Zapatistas is not unconditional. We are not blind followers of Marcos and the EZLN leadership. We are here in solidarity with the base and recognize that the EZLN are compañeros in struggle. This is where Mexico's at, at this moment in time—the coal-face of the struggle—and we anarchists are here to lend our support and solidarity. And despite not having any real role in the decision-making process, we try to give voice to a more emancipatory line."

This pretty much reflects how I see my presence here too. I muse on that fact that, despite our primary aim in Roberto Arenas to build a bridge of solidarity with the indigenous Zapatista compañeros and compañeras, inevitability we end up building really solid bridges of solidarity with *each other*, the caxlan part of the solidarity equation. So it is with me and Praxedis—we are forging a strong comradeship that stretches far beyond this very water project. Although he hails from Mexico City and I from Dublin, we actually share not just an ideological affinity to anarchist thought, but also a somewhat similar political background. And so perhaps it is that that one of the by-products of the Zapatista insurrection is to bring like-minded people together, beyond national frontiers.

Talking of reciprocity, one thing is certain at this moment: our friendship has grown to the take-a-bullet-for-my brother kind of level, and it is a fine thing.

After a long and involved discourse in our rustic kitchen, I propose we need to further sharpen our intellectual guile, so it is time to retreat to the schoolroom for reading by candlelight—the ultimate intellectual indulgence. My aching hands, arms, back, and burnt neck find a little distraction in the monstrosities of Conrad's *Heart of Darkness*. Exhausted, swatting at legions of chaquistas and mosquitoes. A minor sting is underscored by the threat of malaria or leishmaniasis. And this useless (imperialist) mosquito netting that always allows in a few. I muse that we are not in the heart of any darkness because the locals' welcome is like a radiant light, warming us and illuminating our every step. Unlike Conrad's Congo, where the colonialists were under siege, we are protected. The compañeros embrace us—if not yet all the way into their bosom, at least under their wing. Of course, some would say we are merely modern day colonists in disguise, introducing elements of western civilization into the darkest corner of the Lacandon. And maybe they are right. These are the same who would accuse us of being social democrat humanists overseeing some charity works, and again they could be right in the long run. But right now we are under siege not from the locals, but from the military and state, so we must be doing something subversive, anti-authoritarian, and right.

Age Of Christ:
Reflections of a Water Worker

Saturday. Waking at 6 AM, I stumble out of my mosquito netting, and look out over the grey, overcast, Irish-like sky in Chiapas. I feel curiously at one with the universe. Glad day.

Today is the last day, today is the first day. I was born thirty-three years ago today—the age of Christ—and, lapsed catholic that I am, it astounds me that I am still not, metaphorically speaking, crucified. I am pleasantly surprised to still be amongst the living. Let every new day be celebrated.

I drag myself across the grassy village center to our rustic kitchen and attempt to light a fire from last night's embers. It's not catching, so I go outside with a machete and extract some slight shavings from a heavy log. The dexterity required to wield a machete is something that, after years of practice, I'm still acquiring. Adding these shavings, I blow on the ashen embers and the little fire ignites playfully, so I add twigs. The craft of fire making is under-rated—I love it. Building fires and watching the crackling, smouldering glow as it burns.

Flames leaping, it is time to put the water on. Of course there is no tap to fill the kettle yet. If fire is play, fetching water is chore: slipping and sliding down the water's edge, filling the twenty-liter vessel, heaving it onto one's shoulder, and always spilling a bit down your back on the way. Then the polluted water has to be disinfected with iodine, one drop per liter. It always feels odd adding a little poison to one's water, but since the water is already poisonous, I shouldn't quibble. Some people can't handle iodine at all, and refuse it. These are usually the kinds of people who refuse to use cell phones or wireless Internet, so there's not a lot that can be done to accommodate them. Still, I think history will absolve them. For now, the water is treated and ready to go. In the trusty old rustic pot, black with soot, sitting like a martyr amongst the dancing flames, it is soon boiling gently.

Sitting quietly at the kitchen table, sipping the first luxurious cup of coffee of the day, listening to the gentle hum of the pastoral community, I hear children's voices, bees buzzing, snorting pigs, crowing cocks, a river flowing by, birds twittering, hens cackling, insects humming, the chopping of wood, a mother calling out for her child, a bird calling into the forest, the crackle of dry firewood on the stove, and a pen scratching the page—mine. The pastoral harmony is disturbed by the distant and unusual sound of tires crunching over the gravel road on the other side of the river. Maybe a military vehicle or a logging truck? No, it sounds lighter, like a new 4WD or pickup truck. Maybe the Red Cross. It passes.

Praxedis appears. After his pre-dawn exercises, he had gone for an early morning swim in the river. He looks refreshed and sharp, ready to tackle the day ahead. I, on the other hand, am grumpy before my second coffee and probably look like I could do with a holiday. It strikes me that, despite my thirty-three years on earth, I own nothing, and this rough kitchen is as much my home as anywhere else in the world. Fifteen years ago I remember me and my fellow teenage brigands graffitied a slogan on some wall in Dublin: "Sometimes you can win by throwing it all away" (with the appropriate anarchy symbol there within), and it seems somewhat far-sighted now. I have thrown away my privileged upbringing and disregarded the prudence of my parents who saw an architect or businessman in me. Fancifully enough, my mother thought I would make a grand captain in the army. Well, here I am no longer young, the age of Christ—important for ex-Catholics and Jesuit boys like me—and it's not quite the placid and un-engaged Irish army that I am submerged in at the moment. Indeed the ragged Zapatista peasants passing the hut with their jovial salutations, a tilt of the ever-present machete, are clearly not what my mother had in mind when she conjured up images of smart military men in spotless uniforms. We are only born of our parents, I concede, reflecting upon the wisdom of my years, we do not become them, or fulfill their ambitions. Although I always remember my good father lamenting (usually after a bad day at work) that he had kids instead of sailing around the world. He liked to write too. Maybe I did realize *some* of my parents' aspirations in the end.

So here I am today, the age of Christ and, if not yet crucified, at least (if one wants to be alarmist about it) holed up in a little rebel hamlet surrounded by 40,000 heavily armed and dangerous soldiers of the Mexican Armed Forces ready for the order to wipe us off the face of the earth. How the fuck did I end up here?!

Like other people, I came to Mexico to die or be reborn. At twenty-nine I felt there was nowhere left to go. Well there were a million other places to go, but only one that had the Zapatistas, a revolutionary movement that didn't speak with a corpse in its mouth. If hope remained, if something existed worth fighting for, if there was somewhere where people had a vision at the end of the millennium, it was here, at the ragged edge of the world itself—the desert of solitude—with the indigenous, the truthful ones, the EZLN.

I wanted to leave behind the old world and recreate myself in a new one. I was tired and weary and felt rendered useless by my own world. Dublin, where I was living at the time, seemed alien, and I wandered around as if in a bad dream, haunted by the past and frustrated by the present. I drank lots of Guinness with cronies and was full of spite and bitterness towards the nascent Celtic Tiger flourishing all around us, the beginning of the Irish neo-liberal wet dream.

There had been great times in Ireland during the early '90s when there was hope of a radical change—little projects and initiatives that held the kernel of a subterranean spring, a possible antechamber to something else. We, the anarchists and fellow-travelers, wanted to live in a different world, passionate, honest, just, free, and sane. We tried, we fucking tired, to change ourselves and the things around us; we brought people together, we created free spaces and ran cafés and bars and clubs and organized beyond our peer group. But everything just seemed to be sucked up into the economic boom, and everybody became mesmerized by all of Ireland's new wealth and capital and forgot about solidarity and collectively building communities based on hope and reciprocity. As I packed my bags, people were coming and going, talking of buying property and houses and cars and holidays in Thailand, and careers in IT, and I couldn't get on that fucking runway quick enough.

I'm quite aware of the quasi-imperialist antecedent for this kind of impulse. Discontented young European males throughout history have being setting off to peripheries of the globe in search of adventure, riches, or salvation. Typical of this class are Marlow, the narrator, and Kurtz, the protagonist, in *Heart of Darkness*. I prefer to position myself among the ranks of people like B. Traven, self-exiled political actors who come unburdened by urges of conquest. To be honest, a sense of fate or a collective impulse of delight led me towards Chiapas. I wanted to participate in this great social upheaval; I wanted to be part of a revolution, and the EZLN had signalled their clarion call. Politically it made sense to go there and give a little push to the effort. The avalanche of powerful and poetic communiqués penned by Subcomandante Marcos seduced a multitude of radicals across the globe, me included. Theory and practice merged in the Zapatista call—praxis became reality in this nowhere place called Chiapas.

That is only the story of how I arrived in the tempestuous mountains of the south-east and threw my lot in with the Zapatista cause, not how I arrived here, more specifically working on water projects. That journey was born of the fire of experience in Chiapas, or a song of innocence and experience.

Full of revolutionary fervor, I decided I was going to throw myself in at the deep end by going to live in a Zapatista base community, as far away and hardcore as I could find, or that would have me. While the social life of San Cristobal was very enticing, with a lively party and night-life scene populated by a somewhat glamorous global revolutionary set, it wasn't what I had come to Chiapas for. And so I washed up in the defiant Zapatista community of Diez de Abril and took up residency as a long-term solidarity activist and *campamentista*.

Accompaniment is a strategy for solidarity activists to engage with the Zapatista base by living alongside them in the communities. They share day-to-day living and, in a sense, leave behind their positions of privilege and sink into the indigenous rural life. What use is a degree in Sociology or computer engineering when a

machete is put in your soft hand and you have to go out and weed the milpa? As a strategy of solidarity, accompaniment is good as the actors work together, finding a common ground "that fosters diversity and decentralization without reinforcing hierarchical relationships between those helping, and those-to-be helped."[8]

It was a busy year in Diez de Abril with two violent military incursions, community resistance to the army invasions, people imprisoned, internecine fighting between local Zapatistas and lots of intrigue. I busied myself around the rural community doing this and that, helping with the new rabbit rearing project, working on the coffee harvest, installing compost latrines, hosting delegations, teaching the little kids football, and sending out blistering reports to a world not at all interested in the momentous happenings in this tiny indigenous village at what seemed like the ragged edge of the universe. Sometimes I felt like an errant parish priest visiting sick Doña Petrona with tamales and a cheerful smile, or taking care of the two little orphaned boys whose mother might or might not have gone away forever, no one seemed to know. Other people from the Irish solidarity group came to stay and there was a tangible sense that we were constructing a solid bridge of solidarity between our Irish-based group and the community. However, despite the great learning curve, the wealth of experience, and the growing relationship with the community, none of us could afford it in the long term.

I declined the compañero's offer of a milpa to support myself. I am not a peasant, nor am I an NGO operative prepared to work for any formal group for the security of wage and institutional support. I am a revolutionary, and that means I endeavor to place myself as much as possible outside of the capitalist wage-slave system! I undertook annual sojourns to wealthier climes to work and fill my coffers with enough loot to see me though the rest of the year as a revolutionary gadfly in the Zapatista zone—an unsustainable strategy. One could stay there for six months, or even a year, but beyond that, to remain required a complete immersion in the campesino lifestyle. A bridge too far. And indeed, while some other caxlan activists remained within the communities for years on end successfully, I learned my own limitations after about a year and a half.

---

8. Marianne Maeckelbergh, *The Will of the Many* (London, Pluto Press, 2009), p. 176.

While submerging oneself into a Zapatista community is a good thing to do, I decided it was not the best approach for me to take, in terms of being a useful player in the greater scheme of things.

Following other people's example, I shifted perspective from accompaniment solidarity to practical solidarity. The political concept of accompaniment was based on the sound premise that we need to move on from the colonial assumption that these poor third world people need our help and we are here to provide aid, to the more enlightened and emancipatory notion that there is a common social and political capacity and we seek it out through struggling side by side. Accompaniment in Chiapas was tactically successful throughout the late '90s, as the presence of caxlan solidarity might well have staved off the worst of the military excesses, serving as eyes and ears to monitor human rights in the conflict zone. However, in consolidating the rebel project of building autonomy, accompaniment was lacking—it was a response to more immediate goals rather than long-term structural strengthening of the revolutionary project.

Practical solidarity was, as the idea suggests, more concrete. It developed by merging the concept of accompaniment with the practicalities of development. Establishing a common purpose between two other seemingly disparate agents, outsiders and indigenous could work shoulder-to-shoulder, recognizing differences and each according to their own capacity. There are many precedents—picking coffee in revolutionary Nicaragua, for instance—but in Chiapas most on-the-ground national and international solidarity seemed to get funneled into accompaniment work in the established peace camps.

Water projects were up and running, and some of my good friends like Maria and Praxedis were already stuck in, so I joined up as a volunteer waterboy. It was a good "solidarity career" move. And so here I am working on my sixth project.

I'm not going to bother telling anyone that it's my birthday. And it doesn't matter that it's the age of Christ—a wholly insignificant signifier in this day and age. That was a long time ago. The "Age of Christ" in the revolutionary milieu would rightly be considered thirty-nine. Emiliano Zapata, Che Guevara, and Malcom X all fell at that age. So I have a few years yet to entertain my revolutionary Thanathos complex. But this is all neither here nor there. Today is a birthday, slightly more noteworthy than the previous ten, and the forthcoming ten, but nevertheless I recognize it with nothing more than Yeats's salient epiphany, "In balance with this life, this death."

•••

After three weeks of intense digging, the men have decided not to work on the trench today. The water has arrived at the gate of the community and finally they can take a day's rest. Nevertheless, a few are finishing their leftover quotas. And inevitably Don Sisifo has rounded up a few willing hands to go back and rework some of the difficult sections—swampy or rocky terrain that was done collectively but not very well.

So I'm just sitting here at the table in this quaint makeshift kitchen, drinking coffee, scribbling away, delighted that we have no work to do today, and whatever about missing out on the fucking Celtic Tiger and my lack of worldly possessions, or even wisdom. I am still bright-eyed, idealistic, romantic, and love being here, at the ragged edge of the universe, on this very day.

I decide to get busy and dig a hole to bury the plastic and other shite that can't be recycled or burnt. There is remarkably little rubbish here, in the absence of supermarkets and consumer culture. It mostly consists of a few empty rice bags, bottles of bleach, and the occasional plastic wrapper. I manage to break the spade in the process—not sure whether it is because of my newfound strength, my clumsiness, or cheaply manufactured materials, but there goes another tool, and we have scant to begin with. I then clean the kitchen, cook, and fetch more water from the stream. During a long, heavy downpour, I retire to a hammock in the schoolhouse and read. Oh my beautiful book of resistance and revolt, *The Bridge in the Jungle by* B. Traven. Praxedis has hardly stirred from his hammock all day; he is deeply entrenched in political philosophy books—Ricardo Flores Magón, Rudolf Rocker, such like.

Alfredo seems asleep when I go to his house around lunchtime to hang out with him and his family. I'll come back later, I say, in response to the groggy voice through the wooden wall. Glad there are other lazy fuckers around the place. Don Sisifo goes off fishing and he takes his rifle for hunting on the off chance that a wild boar or mountain cat comes his way by the remote riverbank. The girls of the house spend all day at the river, washing clothes, bathing, and playing around. Horsemen ride by.

Idle curiosity or else a sense of foreboding brings me out in the late afternoon to check the water flow from the pipes. This conscientious act—on a Saturday to boot!—is rewarded by the discovery of the worst possible plumbing news: the flow is halved! The pipes are way too light when I pick them up. Fuck!—a leak, a hole or an air-block! A faulty connection, something fucked up, and at moments like this one's mind tends to run riot: Is the water system completely ruined? Is there some fundamental flaw and it has all been a terrible waste of time? Rushing back to the community center I bump into Gordo.

"Are you OK?" he asks. "You seem in a hurry."

"There's a problem with the flow in the pipes, but I'm sure it will be fine. I'm going to get Praxedis and sort it out."

"Maybe just turn the globe valve open to the full," suggests Gordo.

"Yeah," I say, "that could be it." I need to relax. He is probably right. It is all fine, under control.

I grab Praxedis, swinging gently in his hammock, relishing the prison writings of Flores Magón.

"Fuck it, man. The water flow is halved. We have a crisis! Come on!"

Praxedis jumps up with his usual military discipline and ideological zeal.

"Let's go!" he says and jogs out the door.

We rush along the line apprehensively. The pipe is half empty the whole way. Fuck. Now we are doomed, and things have been going so well. What could it be? We slowly inspect each segment of pipe and each connection. The pipe is light and therefore almost empty, the whole length of the line. No signs of leaks or holes anywhere, so the problem must be up at the spring. All sorts of fears cross our minds. What if we worked out the head wrong, and there are air-bubbles in the system that will make it permanently unworkable? We inspect the spring box carefully: the tap looks fine. We uncover the mesh wire protecting the entrance. Fuck! There's a big chunk if wood jammed in the mouth of the entrance pipe! How did that get through all our various defence walls and layers of mesh, wire, and net? Bizarre. Would a kid have shoved it there to fuck it up as a joke? No, that can't be it. Would somebody have tried to sabotage the system? No, that's inconceivable too. Somehow this chunk of wood got through a hole in the defense walls and wire netting and got sucked into the tube entrance. Quite bizarre.

With a great sense of relief, we remove the despised object. The water is pulled in by the gravity of the half-empty pipe, and after a bit of farting and gulping, it soon goes full speed into the system. With a spring in our stride, smiling widely, we jaunt back into the community. At the end of the line, open, lying on the side of the ongoing trench, the water is pumping out at full pressure: a liter every four seconds. It's mended! If there was a bar in this village, we would go celebrate with a few triumphant beers. Instead we can puff heavily on some filterless Alas cigarettes and tell the story of the chunk of wood again and again to anyone who will listen.

Praxedis plays basketball with the youth in the late afternoon. I write in my journal. The sunset is deep red and resonant. People retire to their darkening huts, lighting candles. The animals of the day—hens and dogs and horses—are replaced by the sounds of the animals of the night—crickets, frogs, cats, the occasional monkey in the distance. The night sky envelopes us, black and brooding; no moon tonight. My birthday, the day of Christ, has passed. I'm working on a water project and I'm feeling good.

Here in the deep jungle, dreams filled with life and memory and potent desire come easily. The solace of this place and the satisfaction of the physical work induces dreams pungent, historic, and rich.

Trench Warfare

Back at work, laying the pipe to the village. We are on the cusp of the distribution tank location; we are almost there and everyone's excited. We connect the last three and a half pipes (350 meters) ignoring the trench, and just running it along the ground. The trench is bogged down for a hundred meters with knee-deep swampy sludge because of the near-impossible digging conditions—every shovelful extracted fills with slush immediately. In a big budget operation we would build a bridge over this swamp for the pipes, but here we have to make do with the cheapest option. The men decide to do the stretch collectively, battling through it foot by foot, together.

"With twenty-three men we will do it in a few hours!" says a smiling Don Sisifo, as if relishing the task. Damn, he would have made a great British officer during WWI. Over the trenches, chaps!

These men like to work. They bounce their energy off one another and work as an enthusiastic team. They are buzzing, and their comradery is tangible. A bunch of men without myriad confusions, hang-ups, bravado, or rivalries between them. Strange. I don't know what it is exactly that is so refreshing to be around, but I do know that this whole project is a big deal for the community. The water system will mean much more than just the women and children not having to carry water for a kilometer on their heads over a slippery treacherous mud track, or an improved supply of water all around— it represents the consolidation of this rebel community. A concrete and pipe representation of all that rebel autonomy means. This is significant. These people have never had piped water in their lives, never had the simple pleasure of turning on a tap in one's own home and have water gushing out.

Praxedis and I get stuck-in with the picks—that fine, capable tool—digging into the moist earth, hacking chucks out and throwing them to the side of the emerging ditch. I like the weight of the pick in my hands. It feels like an extension of my body, comfortable, exquisite, and powerful, even if it is not. (We should have a fucking JCB backhoe here digging the ditch. Now *that's* power!) The earth is unusually soft. It feels rich to dig into, even though it is quite a violent act, tearing at the earth surface. This earth receives our tools generously, like a caress of the surface. Not all violence is destructive. Although, as I work it, it feels like this pick is doing me more damage than I do to the earth.

The long dig is almost complete. The last hundred meters of pipe is left out of the trench, bypassing the work in progress temporarily. It carries the water all the way to the community. Piped to the site of the tank, at the highest point in the community, the flow of water is good. Praxedis and I pull on our engineering caps again and hold one-liter water bottles under the flow to time how long it takes to fill: over one liter every four seconds. That means there is a sufficient supply for everyone. It's that simple.

It is all smiles and pride as the water arrives in the heart of the community. Women come out to fill their buckets. A young compañera, dressed in de rigueur colourful dress with shiny plastic adornments and stuff in her hair, approaches cautiously and eyes the gushing pipe lying in the grass.

"Can I?" she asks, timidly. Of course! She fills her bucket, and sips the water in the palm of her hand with apprehension. She flashes us a big smile, "It's good!"

And so she is saved the hike to the river. Next, some emboldened children wander up and begin washing their hands and faces with the water. Yes, it's for real: water is arriving! There's a sense of excitement building. Vicente presents us with a large pumpkin from his garden, a gift of thanks.

"It really means a lot to us," he says. "We are a young community. We can count on having a church, a basketball court, a canoe, and now water."

We accept his gratitude with suitable humbleness.

"Can you help us with building a hammock bridge across the river?" he asks.

"We have a lot of work to finish the water system," says Praxedis. "It's only a little over half done! We have a tank to build, and a distribution system. One thing at a time, compa!"

The water system represents stability and permanence for the community. It says, "We are here to stay!" in plastic pipe and concrete, on this occupied rebel territory. We are not squatters; this land is ours!

Later will come the next steps—a concrete basketball court, a cinder-block church, maybe—if they can score a transformer, a lot of cable and a few tall wooden posts—some electricity pirated from the lines a few kilometers away. This is oil-rich Mexico in the twenty-first century, a country of mega-businesses controlled by a cabal of billionaires, and there is almost no electrification in this part of the vast jungle zone. It is a fucking disgrace.

Later, Praxedis and I are sitting outside the school, having a final smoke before sleep, admiring the soft night hues and the buzz of the mountains and forest, when a small group of compas approach. They gather round, accept the proffered cigarettes and, by their sense of purpose, it is clear they have something on their minds.

"We are making good progress, compas."

We are.

Silence. No, they are not here to talk about the progress. There is something else on the compañeros' minds.

Alfredo acts as spokesperson. He clears his throat, sits upright, and begins slowly.

The compas have a question, he says.

Yes?

"How many floors are there in your house?"

Is this a trick question? I mean, I don't have a house. Does he mean the place we rent in San Cristobal?

Single story, I tell him, like most houses in San Cristobal.

"No, no, in your country."

I explain I don't own any houses in Ireland, but the last place I lived in, years ago, before emigrating, was a four-story block of flats.

"Four floors!" exclaims Alfredo and tells his cronies. They reply with a mass "*ta' mal!*"

"And you, Praxedis?"

"In Mexico City? Our family house has two floors."

Alfredo nods his head. The compas discuss this news with keen interest.

Why? I ask. What difference does it make?

"We have heard that people are so rich in your countries that they have to build more floors on top of their houses to keep their money."

"Eh, well, figuratively speaking maybe."

"So people like you who live in house with three or four stories are very rich, no?"

No. I try to explain best I can.

It should have prepared me for the next question. It comes, translated by Alfredo, from Enrique and Ricardo, the tall Galician fishermen with beards.

"We have heard of other countries beyond the United States, and Italy and France, Germany. Is your country one of the further countries we have heard of, like Pluto?"

Maybe they are right. Maybe Ireland is as far away from this Tzeltal community in the Lacandon Jungle as Pluto.

Here are men who can identify a dozen different kinds of corn, or know which different seeds will grow in what soil, or raise extended families with very limited resources under very difficult circumstances—all these things I know nothing of, so who am I to mock this worldview?

Nevertheless, it is a satisfying thing to try and explain the Earth and the planets to someone who has not learned much about it before. Like opening up whole new galaxies to someone.

An Unexpected Visitor

"**W**e have a visitor," says Praxedis, waking me in the soft pre-dawn light.

"Who, what, where?" I say, dishevelled by this rude awakening.

"There's a guy chained to our kitchen door."

What?!

"Come see."

I throw on a few clothes and make haste over to the kitchen.

Sure enough, as Praxedis says, there is an unfamiliar man chained to the kitchen door bolt. Nearby, a group of young compas guard him.

The chained man looks petrified and a bit roughed-up.

"What's going on?" we ask the nearest youth.

"Nothing," he says, nonchalantly.

"Who is he?"

"I don't know," says the youth.

"Why is he tied to our kitchen door?"

"Saber? Who knows?" says the compa, unhelpfully.

We are not making any progress here, so we turn to the prisoner.

He is a young guy with a shaved head, black clothes, boots, and several visible tattoos—messy and homemade—on his arms.

Who are you?

"*Puta!*" he groans, as if in pain, or semi-unconscious.

Fuck. This is not good.

When in doubt, seek out Don Sisifo.

His family kitchen is nearby. We knock at the doorway. He ambles out, a man perfectly at ease with the new day. "Don Sisifo, there is some guy tied up outside our kitchen!"

Who? he asks, nonplussed.

"We don't know. Some stranger."

"Oh him," says Don Sisifo, pausing.

Sometimes, I have noticed, the compas can be very elusive when talking about sensitive issues to caxlanes. He resumes.

"He is some stranger. We found him crossing the milpa. We tied him up."

He turns back to enter the kitchen.

"But...eh, can we get into the kitchen to make breakfast?"

"Yes, yes, of course. Let me come over with you."

We return to the kitchen, and Don Sisifo talks to the youths in Tzeltal. They untie the man and lead him off across to the schoolhouse we have just vacated. They tie him to the door there.

"*Vale pues*, alright, let's go to work," says Don Sisifo cheerfully.

"What the fuck is going on, Don Sisifo? We can't just head off to work without knowing what's happening."

He stops and scratches his head.

"Well...OK. It's not that important."

So it turns out that they found this unfortunate guy stumbling about the community milpa last night. They apprehended him and brought him into the community for questioning. Their suspicions were aroused by his military-style boots and shaved haircut.

"We think he could be a soldier."

What does he say?

"First he said he was a *norteamericano* and then he said he is a migrant from Honduras trying to cross the border from Guatemala into Mexico and he got lost. So we don't know. We are going to interrogate him more later."

"I could speak to him in English to see if he is a North American."

"And I can ask him about Honduras," offers Praxedis, who had visited the country.

Bueno pues, fine, agrees Don Sisifo.

So we return to the school. By now, a lot of children and women have come out to see the prisoner and they sit around staring at the unfortunate man, tied up like a chicken on a post. It has become a lively public spectacle.

I approach him and ask him if he is from the United States, in English.

"Yo, homey!" he says, somewhat dubiously.

Where you from, man?

"Yo, homey!" he repeats.

What's up with this guy? Is he delirious?

He is not from the United States, I inform Don Sisifo. And maybe he needs something to eat or drink.

They give him some Coca-Cola. (Now this is torture, I'm thinking. Coca-Cola, for fuck's sake.)

Praxedis starts to ask him about Honduras, and he responds more promisingly to this line of questioning. He has a Honduran accent, Praxedis tells the assembled.

Then he takes a closer look at his tattoos. Mara 18 (or Mara Salvatrucha 18) predominates.

"Yes, definitely Honduras, a gang member. Not a soldier. Not military," announces Praxedis.

"How about his boots and his shaven head, like a military cut?" asks Sisifo.

"All the gang members have shaven heads," explains Praxedis. "And if the guy is attempting to walk from Honduras to the US border, well then he needs good boots for sure, right?"

Don Sisifo relates all this information in Tzeltal to the assembled—including all the men on their way to work on the trench, who are now all gathered around. A debate strikes up and everybody has a lot to say, including some women, who we hear talking in assembly for the first time. It quickly develops into a tumultuous meeting, and while it is fascinating to witness community justice in action, we have no idea what is going on because it is all in Tzeltal.

"What's happening, Gordo?" we whisper, on the fringe.

"They are deciding what to do with the stranger," he explains. And that is all he is giving away.

After an hour, the debate shows no sign of abating, the sun is rising high in the sky and I'm feeling it for the poor guy, still strung up on the post, awaiting resolution on his fate.

Praxedis and I, realizing that our presence is neither helpful nor necessary, decide to relocate ourselves to the construction site of the distribution tank. Having already made level the site, we measure out a three-meter circle with string and a stick, and mark it in the ground. Then we dig a shallow trench outside the circle, filling it with rocks. This will serve as an outside foundation for the tank.

It's ready to be filled with cement. I am excited because it is the first time we are using cement in this project! I generally hate concrete but, inexplicably, I like mixing up cement. Maybe because it is something I can do well... There's a good feeling in constructing things.

The compas return to work, and join in the cement mixing. It is something they are all good at, having at some time or another worked on construction sites outside of the community.

So after an hour of mixing and filling the circular ditch, I am somewhat proud of this little tank foundation. Noticing my pleasure at the job, the compas scratch "Don Ramon's ditch" in the setting cement. I don't mind them teasing me gently, and it's a good sign: I'm not going to get tied to a tree yet.

Around midday we break for matz, and Praxedis and I bring up the situation of the stranger.

"So what happened?"

"He is a migrant going north. The community are going to help him on his way through the region."

Well that comes as a relief! And so the predicament passes. I am delighted that no further misfortune will befall the stranger in this community. Despite a satisfactory outcome, the whole situation did reveal a rather atavistic side to the system of community justice.

It is not always so brutal. I remember the time in one community when we were witness to the case of a young miscreant who was caught stealing a chicken from his neighbour, a hard-working single-mother raising three kids. The matter was taken very seriously. The teenager was locked up in the community jail, the justice commission adjourned, and most of the village gathered to discuss the issue in the community church. People came and went all day long, giving their account of the incident or testimonies on behalf of the boy. The single mother demanded swift punishment and compensation for the missing chicken. The father of the offender offered to replace the chicken with one from his own stock, but the woman refused, claiming the scrawny looking offering was diseased.

She demanded a cash reimbursement. Eventually, after eight long hours, the justice commission—comprised of three men and two women—ordered the boy to do five days of community service, which meant clearing the collective milpa, and the lady was ordered to accept his father's scrawny chicken and 30 pesos compensation, to be paid by the boy or his family immediately. Everybody left the church satisfied that justice had been served. A few days later, the lady, her anger assuaged, invited the youth to dine with her family. The youth brought a 2-liter bottle of Coca-Cola as an offering of, I don't know...peace, or maybe as a kind of apology. It was a nice conclusion to the whole episode that served to emphasize the rehabilitating nature of this kind of community justice.

Meanwhile, back on site, we are ready to lay the concrete foundation for the tank base, but we need a sizeable quantity of gravel and sand. To lay a solid three-meter circular floor with a five-inch-thick base, firm enough to support the 13,000 liter cement tank, we need a lot of sand and gravel. Don Sisifo brings us up the hill to an abundant source of fine sand, and another pit filled with stonier sand, which he hopes could be used as gravel.

"This soil is way too sandy," says Praxedis, the gravel expert, "we need well-formed gravel."

So off we go, deeper into the hills, on a treasure hunt. We cut our way through the woods with machetes. There is better gravel to be found here but it's still sandy and brittle. We all spread out and search around the hillsides and ravines. As time passes, the variety of soil and earth we encounter in our search is astonishing—in one or another mountain or hill there has been just about every variety of soil, sand, and gravel under the sun. From a distance, it just looks like a big fucking contiguous mountain, and yet, this mesmerizing variety I had never even conceived of surrounds us.

Eventually, Praxedis comes across a little ditch with the right kind of gravel. It's not perfect, but adequate for the job at hand. And better to return with something to keep the show on the road. It is a good two kilometers from the construction site, though. Portering time again!

Now these madmen want to carry forty kilos each of gravel, mecopal style, down the steep, slippery hills to the community. Everyone fills their sack and slings it over their shoulders. I can hardly lift the fucking sack off the ground. Two compas hoist it on my back, and we set off together down the treacherous, muddy path in a long single line, like a mule train. Each and every man carries a full bag, young and old alike, from the fifteen-year-old boy Juan to the somewhat-elderly Don Job, and Praxedis and I too, all doubled over with this weight on our shoulders and back, held by a rope around our foreheads. It takes a lifetime to learn how to do this properly, this portering extravaganza, and I, for one, am struggling. My back has never endured such weight for such a distance before. It feels dangerously strained.

Doubled over, the rope around my forehead slips and, for a moment I panic, fearing I'll be strangled by the noose attached to the weight on my back. I stumble, then slip, and finally, go flying off the track, and fall heavily into a ditch. As I sit there, dazed and scratched and bruised, I am overwhelmed by one thought: well, that's it, it is all over, I will never walk again.

The gravel has burst forth from my sack and lies in a pitiful heap all around me. I feel like crying.

"Are you OK, Ramon?" shouts out one of the compas.

"Yeah, I think," I mutter, disconsolate.

I feel about my body but nothing seems broken, a good sign.

And the compañeros don't even stop their portering procession to help me onto my feet and sympathize with my near-death experience! They just keep trudging on under the substantial weight on their backs. And they are all laughing. Laughing! I mean it must have looked spectacularly hilarious to see the gringo fall head over heels into a ditch, but lads, this is the stuff of paralysis, not a merry slip on a banana peel.

To add to my shock, I am now pissed off to boot too. How dare they laugh! I could have fallen and rolled down the steep incline just over there and killed myself! Instead of a little consideration and maybe a mite of compassion, all the men laugh at my clumsiness.

Appalled, and fuming, I pick myself up, dust myself down, check each limb again carefully, and refill my sack. Somewhat sheepishly, I have to leave a few shovelfuls of gravel out, and I give up on the mecopal idea completely. Alone, I plonk the far more manageable half load on my right shoulder. I seethe quietly every step of the way, cursing gravel, slippery mud, and the men who mock me.

I arrive back at the construction site and all the men are sitting around recovering. Now I waltz up, the last one, looking miserable with my puny little half-full bag and it's again cause for great mirth for all and sundry. I am livid by the time I empty my gravel onto the sizeable heap, as a crescendo of laughter fills the air. Praxedis is laughing too, and now I feel betrayed, as well, on top of everything else. Really, I'm fit to pack my bags and head over the mountains to go back to Celtic Tiger Ireland and get a job in a library. Right fucking now.

Instead I take a deep breath. The ridiculousness of pride. Of things that don't matter.

"OK, compas let's go," I say. "Second round!"

They all laugh again, but this time... They are laughing with me.

This intolerable workday comes to an end moments later as we realize it's late, well past 3 PM, and so the workday is over. Everyone tramps back into the community exhausted.

The End of the Tether

The Honduran drops by our kitchen at breakfast the next day. He looks a lot better now that he's not all tied up. He saunters in, full of attitude, and he speaks with that cool, affected drawl of the street.

"Yo homies, I'm taking off now," he says, "but I wanted to drop by you guys before I hit the road."

He and Praxedis hand-slap in some complicated, esoteric routine of chic touching and clicking of fingers. I shake hands with him the traditional way, and feel very unhip.

"Cool to have met you," says Praxedis. Even if the circumstances were a bit Monty Python, I'm thinking.

He tells us he is indeed walking to the USA—although he will ride trains and hitch when possible.

How does he feel after his ordeal here?

"No problem, it's all good," he says. "The compañeros gave me food and shelter like good Samaritans, and have told me the path to the north. Respect."

And the initial, ehm, misunderstanding?

"Oh that's chill; I totally understand why they would detain me. I was an intruder in a warzone, crossing their patch. They have told me about the Zapatista rebellion and their beef with the motherfucking state and military. I never heard of them before or their struggle, but I reckon they are kind of homies like us at war with the state, but from the campo!" he says, putting the pieces together.

"Yeah man," agrees Praxedis, "same beef, different battlefield. Against the same motherfucking state."

They do another elaborate hand-slap, clicking fingers and they both say alright! *Orale*, for Praxedis, *cheke pues* for the Honduran.

It seems that Mexico City and San Pedro Sula share a similar hip street style.

The two "homies" get into talking about life on their respective mean streets. While Praxedis comes from a rough enough chilango barrio, nothing compares to the violence and wanton mayhem of the streets of San Pedro Sula, Honduras's second largest city. The Honduran tells of an appalling scenario, where the barrios are pulverized on one hand by a ferocious internecine war between the heavily armed street gangs, and on the other by the state security forces' iron fist policies against youth delinquency.

"I joined the Maras," explains the Honduran, holding up his forearm to show a large Mara 18 gang affiliation tattoo, "because if I didn't, I couldn't survive a day in the barrio. You have to affiliate yourself with one or other gang, otherwise you're fucked, man."

He uses two fingers to indicate a gun and presses them to his temple.

Nor does he exaggerate. The social war in Honduras has reached astonishing levels of ultra-violence—random buses are shot up by AK-47-wielding thugs and dozens of passengers shot dead, or authorities barricade the exits and burn down cellblocks of imprisoned gang members, killing forty or fifty at a time.

"Everybody in the hood belongs to a gang," explains the Mara. "It's basic survival. There are thousands of gang members in San Pedro. We are everywhere and control a lot of turf in the barrios."

Human Rights Reports quote numbers like 100,000-plus gang members in Honduras. The media present them as some kind of appallingly strung out, violent Frankenstein beast mired in an underworld of hardcore delinquency and crime—and the facts on the ground go some way to support that reading. There are an average of ten homicides daily in Honduras; the crime level is extraordinary. But the other side of the equation is that they are also a product of an incredibly violent society where police and military atrocities are commonplace and state sponsored death squads, formed in the 1980s to eliminate the guerrilla, roam the streets with impunity, gunning down Maras and street kids. The Mara phenomenon is like a pre-apocalyptic manifestation of neo-liberal social and economic catastrophe.

"We are at war with the police, with the state. If they come on our turf, it's to kill us or arrest us, so we gotta defend ourselves," he continues. "Fuck the police, and fuck the system."

Praxedis is warming to the guy: "*Orale!*"

"And fuck everything, fuck it all," finishes the Mara.

"No man, you Maras are one step from being revolutionaries. You need to organize in your barrios and communities."

"Fuck that most of all," spits the Mara. "The only thing we organize in the barrio are drugs. Fuck the neighbors, man. I don't give a shit about anyone. It's about looking after number 1."

Herein lies the deeply ingrained nihilism of this kind of delinquent subculture. They are against everything.

The broader picture in San Pedro Sula is framed by Honduras being pulverized by the global drugs industry. The Atlantic coast of Honduras is a significant corridor in the transportation of hard drugs from Colombia to the USA. Millions of dollars worth of contraband flow through this region every month, and the devastating spin-off is a flood of cheap gear and a flourishing clandestine economy overseen by *narcotraficantes*, warlords, and their private armies. The trickle-down effect of this rancid form of pirate neo-liberal economy is turf war on the barrio level.

Mara Salvatrucha[9] first formed life in the '90s on the streets of Los Angeles, amongst the Salvadoran refugee community, as a self-defense outfit. The Maras came to El Salvador when, from 1998 onwards, in excess of 12,000 gang members were deported from California. The unholy mix of hardened street gangsters who had earned their kudos on the mean streets of Los Angeles with the social disaster of a war-traumatized, poverty-ridden quagmire like El Salvador produced the ruthless gang sub-culture centered around

---

9. Mara Salvatrucha is a term used to describe all gang members whether they belong to MS-13, MS-18, or any of the other Mara offshoots.

well-armed, rap-obsessed, deracinated males (and to a lesser extent, females). It spread like wildfire, clandestine and autonomous throughout the other Central American Republics, offered, not only an identity and meaning for abjectly alienated youth, but also a source of income through organized crime in the form of drug dealing, extortion, and robbery.

We would like to talk to this particular amiable Mara all day, but he has to get going as he has a long journey ahead of him. One last set of questions: Why are you walking to the USA?

"You need to know Honduras well," he said. "The only choices I had were to go to prison and be killed there by the authorities, or be shot by my own gang"—he raises his shirt to reveal the remnants of a ghastly bullet wound—"or get out and head north. I left with nothing, just the shirt on my back."

"How did you end up stumbling around here in he middle of the nowhere?"

"I got completely lost crossing over the mountains at the border."

He pulls out a tattered map which looks like it was pulled out of a school geography textbook.

"Guess my map-reading skills are not up to scratch. Damn, I never even set foot outside of San Pedro Sula before in my life!"

We wish him well, present him with a gift of a map of Mexico which I happened to have packed in my stuff, and off he goes, a pleasant enough character despite the desperate circumstances.

So the next day we begin the cement work to lay the floor for the distribution tank. Teams are set up for sifting the sand, then mixing the gravel and cement powder. Finally, the whole mixture is shoveled into a mound and the water is poured slowly into a little lake in the center. It's left to permeate the mix for a few minutes and then a group of men begin to shovel it all without letting the water escape from the sides. It is hard, labor-intensive work, and my body aches even though we take turns with our limited number of shovels. Yearn for a cement mixer, one of the construction industry's greatest inventions!

A few sweltering and chaotic hours later, a large, thick concrete floor, capable of supporting the tremendous weight of the distribution tank, is in place. We did, however, over-extend the floor a little, using two extra bags of precious cement that took such work to get here. We should be more economic!

And then there is the never-ending tale of gravel and its woes. We made an error the day before up at the gravel pit, calculating that we'd need 800 shovelfuls of gravel for the whole tank and base. We got our calculations wrong—we only need 400. All day, compañeros have been trekking up the mountain and returning with sacks of gravel on their backs. We already have about 200 shovelfuls too much and still it keeps coming. Some bright spark has even thought to bring a horse up and, at this very moment, he's arrived back from the gravel pit. The beast has a double load tied around his saddle.

"Fuck!" say Praxedis and I, jointly. "Please no more! That is more than plenty..."

We are a little embarrassed, trying to think of something, anything to do with the extra 200 spades-full of gravel—a growing mound. We almost drop with fright as yet another couple of horses arrive laden down with tons of gravel.

"We shall use it for something," says Alfredo. "But it has to keep coming."

Each compañero has an allotted quota, and has to deliver it whether it is necessary or not.

"Must comply to the quotas," insists Don Sisifo. And then he himself scoots off up the mountain with his Rocinante to collect his remaining quota.[10] Oh dear, oh dear, the occasional tyranny of collectivisation. This ode to useless labor and the myth of Sisyphus comes to mind.

Myths are made for the imagination to breath life into them. I've always considered the myth of Sisyphus a good analogy for revolutionary struggle, especially anarchism—endless struggle— but here in the jungle and the mountains of the Lacandon, I am getting a whole new understanding of the notion.

. The usual symbolic figure associated with Zapatistas is their namesake, Mexican Revolutionary hero Emiliano Zapata. Sometimes the image of Che Guevera is evoked. And for sure they are both potent symbols for the image of the Zapatistas, or more specifically, the EZLN. But at the risk of introducing another western figure into a distinctly non-western cultural environment, I would draw on the ancient Greek myth of Sisyphus to represent the kind

---

10. Rocinante is the name of Don Quixote's skinny but hardy horse in the novel *Don Quixote*, by Miguel de Cervantes.

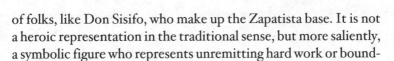

of folks, like Don Sisifo, who make up the Zapatista base. It is not a heroic representation in the traditional sense, but more saliently, a symbolic figure who represents unremitting hard work or boundless endeavor.

Sisyphus was the mortal who challenged the pantheon of Greek gods and for his insolence is condemned to roll a huge boulder up a hill throughout eternity. Each time he reaches the top of the hill, the boulder rolls down again to the bottom. His predicament is usually understood as a metaphor for humanity's futile and ceaseless toil, condemned, at least according to the mythology, to an infinity of punishment and frustration. And so we have the indigenous Zapatista Don Sisifo (not his real name) rolling his rock up the mountain. A life of toil without remittance, his own struggle for survival and for that of his family and community, a Sisyphean task. What sustains him and his ilk?

Albert Camus's 1942 essay, "The Myth of Sisyphus," is helpful here for understanding this dilemma. In it, Camus rejects the standard interpretation of Sisyphus as a tragic victim of a terrible punishment meted out by unforgiving gods. Instead, he imagines Sisyphus as personifying the absurdity of human life in general, in an existential sense. More significantly, Camus's Sisyphus is a hero, though an absurd one.

> He is, as much through his passions as through his torture. His scorn of the gods, his hatred of death, and his passion for life won him that unspeakable penalty in which the whole being is exerted toward accomplishing nothing. That is the price that must be paid for the passions of this earth.[11]

Camus argues that what sustains Sisyphus is the certainty of his fate; having rebelled, he accepts his absurd condition, and the source of his contentment is the notion that "there is no fate that cannot be surmounted by scorn." Camus presents Sisyphus as a proletarian of the gods, one who defies his terrible fate by being conscious and aware of what he is doing and of the need to continue on.

And that is how I envisage this flesh and blood Don Sisifo before my eyes—not as a revolutionary hero like Emiliano Zapata or

---

11. Camus, Albert. 1942. *The Myth of Sisyphus and Other Essays*. New York: Vantage International.

an epic guerilla legend like Che Guevara, but a humble man, a conscientious worker, a rebel, and—in a Camus sense—a proletarian
of the gods.

Unlike me, who is no proletarian, no god, but one who is
tired and weary and ready to leave after only a few weeks of this
Sisyphean life. I desire creature comforts like milk in coffee, freshly
baked bread, fresh fruit, an apple, such things—anything but rice
and tortillas. It's been almost three weeks since I had a beer or used
a computer, and how nice it would be to hear some recorded music!
I am a hopeless urbanite, I conclude, and am like a fish out of water
in the campo. I actually ache for the taste of my favourite snack—
a silly cheese sandwich. And, tragically, I'm thinking maybe I
shouldn't have been so generous with that chocolate bar I gave to
Marisol. It's pathetic. This place is an environmental Shangri-La,
and I'm pining away for my selfish little creature comforts. I doubt
many people here have ever eaten a cheese sandwich.

•••

Amongst a chaotic symphony of slapping cement, the last of the
concrete work, to make the floor level, is done by five madmen.

We just want to make sure the floor is level and fortify the foundations. What if there is an earthquake and the whole thing just collapses? Using strings that don't measure up we attempt to make a flush five-inch-thick cement floor. Is it level? It has to be level— the whole 13,000 liter tank stands on it! I'm not convinced. By 2 PM we have a floor, and a ton of cement that we'll leave for a week to harden before we work more on it. Over goes the tarpaulin to protect it from rain and shine. We are almost done. Everybody is quite content. The compañeros are all fooling about and laughing and joking. I am stressing out unnecessarily.

"Compa, hand me the hammer, please," I say to the young compa near me. He ignores my request.

I repeat myself, a little louder. Again he ignores me, facing the other way.

I have a short fuse today. I feel disgruntled and tired of being here.

Fine, fuck it, I will get it myself, I say grumpily, thank you very much.

The young compa turns to me and smiles sweetly. I push him aside.

"Fuck's sake, Praxedis," I say, fuming. "Sometimes people are really annoying."

"Take it easy, Ramon," he says. "That is Armando. He is deaf and dumb."

Oh shit, I had no idea! Now I am grumpy, tired, and mortified. They must think I am such an asshole!

Here we are, 1,968 meters from the fresh water spring, and before us we have a PVC pipe spouting clean water at a rate of .4 liters per second. We have a five-inch solid concrete base with a good foundation and we are all set. These three weeks, of the eight we'll work on the project, have been very productive. After our work is finished, the people's lives will be changed immensely, and lives will be saved, to boot. It's all good, and I am ready to get the fuck out of here.

It is the last night for this stage of the project, and Praxedis and I will leave Roberto Arenas tomorrow. It feels like the end of a great journey, although we have not travelled far; like the end of an affair, although we have not kissed. We have lived in each other's shadow for three weeks, felt every push and shove, shared the bleeding and sweating and farting and laughing, and all the stories and the tortillas and cigarettes and travails. This is comradeship and it doesn't go away, it won't.

Don Sisifo comes around to the kitchen. He's feeling ill and tired, but remains animated. I can tell he's happy about the progress of the work. I'm sure he wonders upon the occasional ineptitude of the "engineers," but he has the generosity to overlook our shortcomings. We have not fucked up; the system is on course. We just lack confidence, finesse. We need Maria for that. Don Sisifo's grace and manners remain impeccable and his remoteness of character unfathomable.

Later, good Vicente and brothers Ricardo and Enrique (of the beards, the Galician-like fishermen) visit the school. Silence predominates the encounter, as we smoke unfiltered Argentinos, but it is a rich silence of people comfortable with each other. We have worked together, we have seen off the blazing sun and the torrential rain together. This silence is one of complicity. A bottle of sugared lemon water is passed amongst us as if it were rich, soothing whiskey. Little boys and girls run around the schoolroom quietly. There's an intangible strength here. This community is fucking hardcore. One would expect Praxedis to do the chatty, outgoing thing, being a fellow Mexican and all that, but, as ever, he is quieter than me. Shy even. Prince warrior-man is tongue-tied. Alfredo lights a couple more candles but it seems an indulgence— we are not doing anything needing light, just staring into space, smoking, silent, so we blow them out—it's more comfortable in the dark anyhow. Quiet among good people and their demure grace. They have shared everything with us, all they have.

Pirate Evacuation

We depart as we arrive, in an adventure-movie-like scenario of wild animals, canoes, mammoth old trees, and pure Congo-style jungle. This time with a wizened old campesino pirate called Don Gaviero.

We wake on the cusp of dawn, at 5 AM. We get the rustic schoolroom gleaming, its shiny dirt floor and tin roof, its tattered map of Mexico and its mood of serenity. The dawn rises, vast and restless, overwhelmingly majestic. I stand on the threshold looking over the quiet valley, silent, inhaling the divine aroma of the pungent jungle. The sun peeks over the tree tops, for now cool, naked, and blisteringly defined. Enjoying my first coffee of the day, I recall the gaze of the Europeans in the *Heart of Darkness* and how the exotic dawn gave them the hope to carry on. Maybe the tropical dawn of these 500 years should be streaked with blood.

The kids are playing soldiers outside the door, "*a donde vas?*" one says. He is playing the role very sternly. As we set off on our long journey back to San Cristobal, this does not strike me as a good omen. We bid farewell. They ask us to bring back a football and we promise we will.

Around comes Gordo, the occasional teacher, translator, and community intellectual who will be our guide for this trip, and away we stride, into the new morning, into the forest.

This exit strategy involves the river. We are not going to cross the mountain to get to the Zapatista headquarters at La Garrucha, and we are not going to sneak past the military checkpoint on the single dirt road out of the community. We are going to float out of the jungle in a canoe, through the dense forest vegetation, propelling ourselves down lush exotic waterways by paddle. I love it. Congo. Amazon. All of the colonial fucking literature themes in one. It's not the Congo and I'm not Conrad, but the Jataté is a very picaresque, romantic waterway and lends itself to many overtures and much verbosity—I will refrain.

The canoe is a rustic wooden dugout, about thirty-feet long, hulled out of an enormous cedar tree. An impressive river-faring vessel, with this intriguing character, a gristly old campesino boat man and navigator, Don Gaviero at the helm to ferry us out. This old Lacandon pirate, Gordo tells us, has seen a thing or two in his numerous years ferrying the Jataté—a legend in his own lifetime. I can imagine: he is even sporting pirate calico-patterned pants. With us seated up near the bow and Gordo paddling alongside Don Gaviero, the canoe glides slickly through the mesmerizing water. The Jataté is a white water river, with a gorgeous tint of pale jade, shot with turquoise, and slightly muddied with silt. Good for canoeing. And good fishing along this stretch, says Don Gaviero. We rove on downstream, where the river narrows and quickens. The ride becomes bumpy and exhilarating.

Don Gaviero guides the long canoe carefully out of the current into a basin off the bend of the river, and maneuvers alongside a giant, old fallen trunk. There he reaches over and somewhat magically pulls up a huge fish caught on a single line. This fish is the size of a small pig. Great excitement! We all lean forward to see the catch, but this is not a fish. It is an alligator. A baby alligator—but still big and monstrous-enough-looking to frighten the fucking life out of me. I will NEVER bathe or swim on the Jataté again! I had no idea.

Don Gaviero gleefully cuts its mouth off with a machete. Its teeth, piercing this dissected jaw, are strong and sharp and apparently somewhat lucrative in certain local markets. The skin is beautiful—and will fetch a price too. But it can't be eaten—the carcass is bloated after a few days rotting here and things are eating its insides. A pity, they say—fine meat, but it stinks. I can smell the rot from here.

All too soon it is time to disembark. Has it only taken two hours to traverse the Jataté? Shouldn't a river epic like this take months to complete? Don Gaviero bids us farewell with a hearty handshake, and offers us the tip of the crocodile's tail as a memento. No thanks! Off he goes, one more of the colorful characters populating the Lacandon Jungle, a figure that could have appeared in one of Traven's novels. I shake his hand, thanking him, this gristly old pirate and Zapatista.

"And don't worry," he says, his parting words. "If the migra catch you, we'll break you out!"

Back on land, we are met by another compañero—Luis, who hails from some nearby Zapatista community invisible to us, and who will guide us through the forest. He is indigenous, but compared to the compañeros in Roberto, this young man seems more urbane and polished. His clothes are crisp and clean, unlike the ragamuffin appearance of the rustic campesinos deeper in the mountains, and his black military boots are shiny and new. He wears a little black cap with a red star. He speaks perfect Spanish, and engages us with the confidence of one who is used to dealing with caxlanes.

"Ireland, then?" he says to me, with a mischievous smile. "We like the Irish around here. Are you going to teach us to blow things up?"

"No!" I say, startled. "We are here in solidarity with the Zapatistas. To learn about your struggle, not to teach anything."

"Ah, then you are no good to us!" he jokes.

"Us," in this sense, we take to mean the EZLN rather than the Zapatista base communities. This Luis guy is obviously from the military side of things. As we walk, he and Praxedis get into a deep political conversation. The compañero Luis appears to be gently reprimanding Praxedis for the failure of the Mexican left and civil society, beyond Chiapas, to get serious about opposing the bad government.

"We Zapatistas are surrounded here by 40,000 federal troops, compa" he says. "Why haven't the compañeros in DF and the rest of the country organized? They can't leave it all to us."

By his manner of speaking, one can tell that this Luis is probably a Zapatista of some high standing.

"I don't know why, compa," replies Praxedis. "It is the key question. We know that as long as the Zapatistas are isolated and enclosed here in the mountains and jungle, nothing is going to really change on a nation-wide level. But, despite a deep reservoir of support for the Zapatistas all over the country, the people seem to be asleep. It is like they need a spark to ignite a more militant response."

"They need to be more organized, compa," says Luis. "We organized for ten years before we rose up in 1994. Compañeros like you should be working in your own community, fomenting rebellion."

"Yeah, I know, I know," says Praxedis, obviously frustrated by this chiding, which he has heard many times too often. "But it is so hard, compa. The people are against the government, but they are filled with fear, and uncertainly. The impact of neo-liberalism has made people more self-interested and there is less social solidarity than ever before. With so much economic precarity, people are first of all looking after themselves and their families."

"That is not good, compa," says Luis. "But one can't despair. We must continue organizing, against fear and against uncertainty. Fear must be turned around into rage. Revolutions are made from such uncertainties. There is no alternative."

We follow a rough trail along the riverbank. The river at this point is broad and majestic. It is rough going and Luis and Gordo have to employ their machetes to effectively clear a passage. Much of the time is spent crawling under huge fallen trees or clambering over slippery rocks. Following a trail unperceivable to me, we turn inwards, heading deeper into the vegetation. The air is fertile with the vitality of the rainforest. We move among trees the breadth of a printing press and the size of 2,000 books stacked on top of one another.

The two compas, Luis and Gordo, stop by the side of a particularly beautiful, enormously tall tree. We gaze awestruck at such a majestic creation.

"Good for a canoe," says the campesino. With a sparkle of delight in his eye.

A canoe, I repeat, yes quite.

So we rove on, slipping and clambering and scraping through the forest, and finally, a couple of hours later, we emerge into the flat land of an extensive milpa. The sudden change is bizarre. It is as if someone has just taken a ruler, drawn a straight line and ended the rainforest at this point, and from here on in, all the way to Ocosingo, it is agriculture. We march along a trail over undulating hills planted with cornfields and on to vast plains. This was once jungle. I shudder to think just how recently this has all been levelled. Praxedis is a pessimist: this whole forest is doomed, it will be gone within a generation.

"Better to slash and burn it now for milpa, rather than one indigenous family go hungry," he says. "And before the big companies get to it for cattle ranching or logging."

It does seem hopeless, a race against time. Who will cut it down first?

The compa Luis makes to leave us at this point—we are on a clearly defined path through the fields, safe and sound. The road is over there, he points, on the other side of the community. Over the hill we can see a cluster of rural houses, and despite their PRI-ista affiliation, Luis assures us it shouldn't be a problem. Just smile, he counsels. But having seen how a stranger was received in Roberto, I wonder is there a possibility that this community might want to tie us to a tree?

Gordo assures us that we will have no such problems here. "Despite being PRI-ista, they are good people."

He explains that he is related to some of the families, and furthermore, he elucidates, he is hoping that they will come back to join the "organization." According to Luis, this community was pro-Zapatista in '94, but changed affiliation a couple of years later. The local PRI officials offered the community help in getting electricity and building materials, and the village assembly accepted. Now, a few years later, they feel that the local PRI authorities are once more neglecting them and they have again approached the Zapatistas.

"Does is happen a lot that communities switch political affiliation?" I ask.

"Sometimes," replies Luis. "It depends on what the people think is best for the community."

Praxedis looks concerned. "Are you suggesting, compa, that there is no political or ideological loyalties involved? That it is simply a question of economics?"

"No, compa. You have to understand how much pressure the communities are under. It is not just the lack of resources and money. The strategy of the military, or the government it represents, is to divide the organization and the communities. Their strategies are to provoke fear through intimidation and harassment, so they can divide the community, and weaken the organization."

"So the shifting allegiances are not just opportunistic?"

"Not really," replies Luis. "Just sometimes they are a little bit opportunistic in the sense that communities stop being Zapatistas for a bit in order to accept government support, and then return to the organization later."

"And the organization allows that?" asks Praxedis. "It seems a little bit unprincipled."

"Well, compa, sometimes the organization doesn't have the capacity to help the communities. We lack resources. The government has all the resources and money in the world to throw at Zapatista communities to try to make them leave the organization. The organization recognizes that the pressure on the communities is very heavy. But I must go," he concludes. "I have to attend a meeting now. And *animo*, compañeros, spirits up! Keep working and organizing, don't lose faith!"

He shakes our hands farewell.

"And you," he says, turning to me. "Tell your Irish compañeros to be ready. Some day we might need their expertise!"

And on that ominous note, he turns on his heels and disappears swiftly back into the forest.

"Do you think he's serious, Praxedis?" I ask. "That the EZLN might resume the armed struggle some time?"

"I don't know, compa. Maybe in self-defense, or a worst case scenario. I think it depends on what the military and government decide to do. Certainly it wouldn't be wise for them to launch another armed offensive, not when it is the government who has all the arms."

Contemplating such terrible scenarios, we finally walk into the PRI-ista hamlet. Just as Luis said, the people in this community are quite welcoming; everybody wishes us a "*buenas tardes*" as we pass through. An older, somewhat respectable couple invites us in for a coffee.

"This is the house of my uncle," Gordo tells us.

It is a well-built house, with a cement floor and, in comparison to what we saw in Roberto Arenas, proper furniture—even a fridge.

The couple are very friendly. As we chat about the weather, the journey, and our job as "water engineers" from an NGO, they ask us could we look at their water system, which has been giving the community problems of late.

Sure.

We stroll over to a very large government-constructed water tank located a little outside the community. It seems enormous— about 50,000-liter capacity—for a small community, not much larger than Roberto Arenas.

"Why did they construct such a big reservoir tank?" I ask.

"They think that because our community is located on the road to Ocosingo, the community will grow a lot over the next few years."

"Maybe they have plans to clear out the communities deeper in the jungle," suggests Gordo.

"That is what some people say," agrees his uncle.

The water tank is an impressive structure—square, and built in the shape of a Mayan temple. The engineering and design is elaborate and quite complex. Peering at the array of pipes and connections, we realize that this is way out of our plumbing league. It is apparent that special tools are needed to even work on it.

"I think you need a professional engineer to look at this," says Praxedis.

"We asked the municipality to send out an engineer six months ago but they continue to ignore us. The community has had no water this whole time."

Well this at least emphasizes one of the advantages of working at the scale we do. If the tank in Roberto malfunctions, the community themselves can most likely fix it. This is a sophisticated system that can only be overseen by specialized technicians who don't appear to be readily available.

Praxedis suggests talking to the junta at the autonomous municipal headquarters in La Garrucha. Sympathetic engineers from the Mexico City-based Luz y Fuerza electrical workers' trade union often give workshops and carry out solidarity work in the Zapatista zone. These professional engineers would certainly be able to make a better evaluation of the problem than us, and maybe even have the technological skills to fix it.

"We should go talk to them," agrees Gordo's uncle. This act would also set in motion a process of reconciliation between this prodigal community and the organization.

A younger man appears on the scene and lingers suspiciously in the background, watching us without saying anything. I'm hoping he is not some government agent or something. Damn, this occupation can make one quite paranoid.

Gordo suggests we make a move. We say goodbye to the kind couple and head for the road.

Who was that? we ask Gordo.

"He is the community *agente*. We don't trust him. He is the most pro-PRI-ista element here, and was the first to sell out and bring the PRI into the community. But his supporters represent less than half the community, the majority are still sympathetic to the organization. There could be a division in the community if they re-join the Zapatistas."

"What will happen then?"

"It will be bad. They will have separate authorities. Maybe the PRI-istas will not allow the Zapatistas to have access to water. There are many divided communities in this region and it increases the tension."

There is an old, open-backed truck approaching so we have to bid farewell to Gordo. We shake hands, thank him for leading us here, and tell him we will return in a week's time with the delegation in tow. He reminds us to bring more tools, and with that we climb on to the packed truck. Ocosingo is only a few hours away via this back road and we most likely won't meet any military along the way, though an encounter with the migration post near Ocosingo remains a possibility.

We hang on for dear life and get the usual thrashing on the ride, perched on top of the truck, sitting on the goods as we are. We disembark with the dozen other passengers at a particularly decrepit looking bridge—a couple of logs perched over a deep gully. The truck crosses it slowly as if it could quite possibly crash through the logs at any moment and that's that, end of the road for the trucker and truck. But it gets across and we clamber aboard, nonplussed, on the other side. We approach the dreaded migra post fifteen minutes outside Ocosingo and I crouch on the floor of the truck, concealed by a couple of sacks and a forest of legs. We presume, based on their compliance in hiding me, that all the other passengers are Zapatistas. Praxedis announces that the post looks deserted and all is well. (I was pulled over at this stop some years back by a bunch of beefy security officials who brandished their guns and shoved us around in the dead of night. A scary experience that led to three of us being expelled from Mexico—my second week in the state. But that's another story!)

We pull into Ocosingo, a market town with a population 50,000.[12] It's a pretty awful town at the best of times, and more Zapatistas were killed here during the uprising than anywhere else in Chiapas. After our idyllic few weeks in the jungle, it feels even worse now, with its noise and traffic and fumes and dirt and all the concrete. Back in dilapidated, sad civilization. The contrast is dramatic: both Praxedis and I, despite our excitement to be back in an urban environment once more, have headaches within five minutes.

---

12. Interestingly enough, upon B. Traven's death in 1969, the local government officials named the town Ocosingo de Traven in honor of the famous author. Traven was an anarchist who lived here in the jungle and his legacy has since gone completely unrecognized. The population stood at less than 5,000 in 1969. The cantankarous German anarchist would probably have turned in his grave at the thought of having such an honor bestowed upon him by PRI-ista officials. Ocosingo de Traven reverted back to Ocosingo a few years later— maybe one of the officials actually read some of Traven's ferociously anti-government revolutionary literature.

III.

Heart of the Community

"The task is endless, it's true. But we are here to pursue it ... We must mend what has been torn apart, make justice imaginable again in a world so obviously unjust, give happiness a meaning once more to peoples poisoned by the misery of this century."—Albert Camus, 1968

Road Hazards and Group Psychosis

The bigger questions of solidarity—like how to radically transform imperialist power relations and create a horizontality of relations on the ground—are at this moment subsumed to more immediate problems of accountability and absence.

"Where the hell are the compas?" asks Maria, irritated. And, here, around dawn in the La Garrucha Zapatista autonomous center, I, for one, think she has good reason to be a little pissed off.

The dawn air is chilly and there's no sign of Don Sisifo or any of the compañeros to lead us over the mountain. We need horses and guides. We have a bunch of equipment and materials that are essential to the next stage of the project, and there are eight of us ready to head over the mountain. But with the compas no-show, we are stuck here.

The local Zapatista commander shrugs noncommittally.

"*Quien sabe?*" Who knows? "We sent them a message," he explains. "We spoke to them by radio, and they confirmed they would arrive here last night for a meeting with the junta, and be here to accompany you now. But nobody has turned up."

He then adds, almost as an aside, "We have been having some difficulties with them lately."

But when pressed, he will reveal no more.

So what should we do? Wait? The thought of wasting a day or two here doing nothing is not appealing.

"*Pues, vámonos,*" says Praxedis, fuck it, let's go, pulling on his backpack. He is gung-ho, as usual. Perhaps Maria and I are fretting unduly. In our defense, it has being a shitty day so far—and the sun hasn't even risen yet. We've been pulled over by the military, we are tired, having not slept all night, and some of the volunteers are grating our nerves.

But let's back up. We left San Cristobal last night around midnight, and had to do without sleep because, well, OK there was a party, and dancing and carousing were involved. It is Saturday night after all! So we pick-up the five-strong delegation at the arranged spot, in the wee hours, and take off into the night. Now eight of us are squashed into a Ford pickup truck, with all the water project equipment. We were somewhere around Ocosingo on the edge of the Lacandon Jungle when the trouble began. It was 3 AM and we were dismayed to discover that the migration office—usually closed at that time of night—was not only open for business, but brimming with activity. In addition to migration officers, there were soldiers and dodgy-looking plainclothes officials, who could very well have been intelligence officers. Fuck. They pulled us over and demanded to know where we're going. It's the old familiar cat-and-mouse game. They suspected we that we were Zapatista sympathizers—subversives—going into the rebel zone and breaking the Mexican constitution, but our fig leaf was that we are tourists on our way to the nearby archaeological site of Tonina, an important Mayan location. We were traveling along a public road and it would look bad for the Chiapas authorities, and indeed the Mexican government, if their security forces were seen to be deporting every foreigner on their way to archaeological sites in the Lacandon Rainforest.

So Maria, as the driver, had to do the smiley, chatty tourist routine, engaging with the migration officer who pulled us over. She showed her passport and visa and tried to humor him into letting us pass. Unfortunately, the migration officer called over the military and the plainclothes guys, one of whom was sporting a holstered pistol under his loose jacket. They poked around the cabin and the back of the pickup, somewhat surprised to discover, in addition to the five people crushed into the cabin, another three in the back. They gruffly gathered up all of our passports and took them away for inspection in the office, while a soldier stood in front of the pickup, holding his semi-automatic rifle at battle-ready stance.

This predicament is pretty standard for us at this stage. We travel late at night in hopes that these officials aren't taking their jobs too seriously, and thus won't oversee their posts 24/7. Occasionally, like now, that strategy fails. So we went through the routine of pretending to be tourists or archeologists, and they went through the routine of trying to ensnare us. Which they appeared to have managed because one of our group had forgotten their tourist visa. The officials insisted we couldn't proceed. We requested all the volunteers bring their tourist visas—so this is pretty annoying.

"You will have to return to San Cristobal to get it," says the official. Maria argues vehemently, and meanwhile, the plainclothes operative is poking around the back of the pick-up, going through the various backpacks and materials.

"Why have you got seven shovels?" he asks.

"In case we get stuck in the mud," answers Maria, insolently. "It's a jungle out there."

"These look like military or guerrilla clothes to me," he says, pulling out somebody's pair of black cargo pants.

"It's all the style nowadays amongst the youth," explains Praxedis, mischievously. "The military look is high fashion."

Eventually after much wrangling, they tire of us and allow us to continue on our way. I think it is our cavalier attitude that helps us in these situations. Despite the hairy isolation of the circumstances and the creepy darkness of the roadblock, we are not scared of their uniforms or bully tactics, and they grow frustrated by our nonchalance.

But of course such bravado does not always secure safe passage—there have been many detentions and expulsions emanating from these very late-night checkpoints—but our group, our water project people, have been lucky so far.

So we continue along the desolate mountain roads, passing the turn to Tonina, and head into rebel territory, bumping along the dirt road to La Garrucha, Zapatista headquarters.

We still have two more roadblocks to navigate. The first, a police barracks, is darkened and deserted, so we drive through unhindered. We are not so lucky at the second, a military post just outside Garrucha. Generally, this spot is unmanned between 2 and 5 AM, but alas, tonight they have stationed a late-night guard. Out of the darkness, a soldier appears, beckoning us to stop, while using his gun to indicate that we should pull over.

"Fuck," says Maria.

The soldier taps on the window. He is an innocent looking teenager with shiny cheeks and a camouflage helmet that dwarfs his head.

Maria rolls the window down and somewhat flirtatiously says, "What's going on, handsome?!"

The young lad is clearly shy and somewhat intimidated by Maria, who is ten years his senior and a looker. His hand is slightly shaky as he takes her passport.

"Where are you going?" he asks.

Here is the problem. We are fairly deep in Zapatista territory already, heading down the single dirt road in a canyon that really only leads to one rebel community after another. Usually we say we are heading for Lake Miramar, another six or eight hours along this track, a mystical lake deep in the jungle where few of us have ever been.

Praxedis, sitting beside Maria, intercedes:

"We are crocodile hunters."

"Pardon?"

"Hunters, here to find crocodiles, as well as mountain lions, wild boar, and jaguars."

The soldier boy is clearly confused.

"You have permission?" he asks with uncertainty.

"We are from the United Nations World Wildlife Foundation," says Maria. "And the Sierra Club."

"What do you hunt with? Guns?" he asks, somewhat taken aback.

"No," explains Praxedis, "We are ecologically-aware environmental specialists. We use natural primitivist methods—spears, sharpened stones, traps, that kind of thing."

The soldiers marks all this down carefully in his notebook.

"Fine, go ahead. Have a good trip," he says waving us on.

It is not usually that easy, but still it is a pain in the ass to constantly deal with these checkpoints. Maria is pissed. "He wrote down my details. Now they know we're here." She is a relatively well-known figure amongst the security forces here. Too many years coming and going. Like a rebel cat-of-nine-lives, eventually it catches up with you. They eventually get all their chaotic bureaucracy together and pinpoint you. They got me later, but that's another story.

We pull into La Garrucha as the sun climbed dramatically over the immense canyons that cradle the little picturesque eighteenth-century-like village—a scattering of wooden huts pitched around a grassy meadow. It's a relief to arrive safely after hours of traversing dangerous back-roads. It's a homecoming of sorts, as we are once again embraced by the warm bosom of rebel territory.

El Comandante, the main man, the local Zapatista head honcho, comes down to greet us, and breaks the news to Maria and Praxedis. No compañeros to accompany us. No horses to carry the gear.

Maria, Praxedis, and I confer and decide between the three of us we can probably find our way over the mountain trails, through the rainforest, and into Roberto Arenas. It will be a six or seven hour hike, made more difficult with the delegation who are not used to such arduous treks, but we can do it. The gear is another matter. We decide to leave the various rolls of water pipes, tools, tap stands, and plumbing accessories here for collection by mules later.

Josef steps up at this moment. "I don't think it is right that you three are making decisions without including us."

This guy is the one who has been giving us cause for concern. Every time he opens his mouth to speak, it begins "No!" or "I don't agree." A difficult character, a contrarian, he has been imposing his point of view about everything, despite this being his first time in Chiapas.

"Does everyone want to go to the community?" asks Maria, a little impatient.

"Sofia? Tlaxlocaztla? You, Omar?"

Everyone nods.

"Yes? Good. Let's go."

Knowing Maria a little at this stage, I think she suspects Josef to be one of these white European guys who thinks he knows it all and wants to be in charge. And he needs to understand that if anyone is in charge, it's Maria!

Josef looks disgruntled. "I don't know. I thought we would conduct the delegation like a collective, agreeing everything in a horizontal manner through the correct mechanisms."

"We can have a proper group meeting when we get to the community, but for now you will have to trust us as the ones with the experience here, OK?" Maria says reasonably. Underneath the façade, I reckon, she is ready to throw him into the river.

We set off as the sun rises. The group is giddy with excitement and sense of adventure, particularly the new volunteers. It is pretty standard on the water projects to include as many people as possible, so volunteers are always welcome. As a manifestation of practical solidarity with the Zapatistas, working on a water project is hard to beat. The activist gets to meet the people on the ground, learn about their struggle, lend a hand, and, most poignantly, begin to build people-to-people bridges across social, political, and cultural divides.

The early stages of this water project didn't lend itself so much to having a bunch of volunteers. The unusual remoteness and inaccessibility of the community and the technicalities involved in the first stages—the feasibility study and laying the main line—made it unwise to include them. Volunteers would have been left digging the ditch for two or three weeks solid, and while that has worked out fine in other water projects, not so in this particular one. In truth, after working on a half-a-dozen water projects, Praxedis and I, and Maria (who has probably overseen about a dozen or more now) are somewhat tired of babysitting caxlanes in difficult circumstances, and so prefer to have less people onboard for the early stages. But now we have a sizeable group and it should be fine; the work ahead is constructing the main water tank and building the distribution line inside the community—labor that is overwhelmingly social and (relatively) undemanding. Volunteers are often more trouble and a hindrance than a help in terms of productivity, but we consider them an important component of the whole project because it is part of the duty of solidarity activists on-the-ground to create a space that others can plug into.

Through the water projects we enable people from other walks of life access to the communities, and through that effort, solidarity is built and expanded. Most volunteers on water projects become more inspired about the cause, and so the network grows nationally and internationally. As much as a water project is about delivering clean water to a community who desperately needs it, it is also quintessentially political work, focused on movement building and generating more awareness and also networks to plug into the general Zapatista project. It is one small step in building a new world, or another world. That is why we consider ourselves "revolutionaries" rather than NGOs or charity workers. We position ourselves and our work in a wider context of political and social struggle.

All of the visitors have been drawn here to work with the Zapatistas and are typical of solidarity activists coming to Chiapas. We have an Italian NGO operative named Sofia, a glamorous thirty-something whose group is interested in future funding of water projects. Also in his thirties is Omar, a media activist planning on doing an interactive writing and recording story for an online publication. Like almost every delegation or group of activists who congregate in Chiapas, we have on board a young hotshot academic who is writing a thesis about the indigenous struggle—this particular representative of the breed being Tlaxtlocaxtla, a feisty Chicana from some liberal US university. At twenty-two, she is the baby of the group. Then we have Nebula, a Barcelona-squatter, a dread-locked crusty type who is "down with the Zapatistas and up for an adventure." Finally, there is the already-notorious Josef, a hardcore punky vegan straight-edger and doctrinaire anarchist who is here because he says he agrees with the fundamental tenets of Zapatismo and that his "political position is reasonably close to the EZLN."

Experience tells us that at least half of them will do something useful for the movement or the communities after the whole adventure is done, and the others are basically just revolutionary tourists, or thrill-seekers who will never be heard of again. Useful follow-up work includes organizing solidarity back in their own cities or towns, following up with projects, producing useful media, or simply staying in touch. Fundraising earns extra kudos. It is quite remarkable the amount of volunteers and visitors to these Zapatista communities who promise things and never follow up. Even something simple like complying with the promise to send photos of the kids back to the communities occurs infrequently. I have found that the worst culprits are academics and filmmakers, those most likely to be in it only to get something out of it for themselves. The best are activist types, NGO people, and politicos. But these are the very characters who are the most likely to be the biggest pain in the ass and some are of the cheap-holidays-in-other-people's-misery variety. The unfortunate truth of the matter is that the "movement" has its fair quota of freaks and wingnuts.

But one can't criticize too much a pleasant group of progressive people, filled with good intentions, who are here to help and to participate in something they collectively adhere to, in one sense or another. It is better that they made the effort to be here, to experience a very different reality, than just, for example, head to the nearest beach resort for their Third World kicks.

Conversation flows between Spanish and English, as everybody has at least a little of both—although obviously Spanish has priority. There should be no problems, except there always are. Delegations inevitably become a soap opera unto themselves and this tension leads to factionalism and schism, impacting negatively on the political, social, and cultural experience of meeting the Zapatistas.

Such tensions are apparent early on when Josef—marching off ahead of the rest of the group in some apparent hurry—slips on a tree trunk bridge that spans a small stream and plunges into the water with a splash. I feel an affinity for the guy as I had fallen in at the same spot just a few weeks ago, but he rejects my proffered hand of help, muttering gruffly, "No, no, it's fine."

Omar the media guy, sensing a cinematic moment, has whipped out his hand-held camera to film the incident, and Josef barks at him, "Turn it off, dude!"

Nebula intercedes, "Take it easy, tiger."

Josef looks to heaven, none too subtly muttering "fucking hippies" under his breath, then notices the student, Tlaxlocaztla, scribbling notes.

"Oh, are you entering some epistemological moment into your case study notes?" he asks sarcastically.

"Pardon?" she replies, icily.

Oh dear. The soap opera has begun.

Maria intercedes decisively. "OK, let's go. We have a six-hour hike ahead of us.

You," she says pointing at Josef, "follow me. You don't know the way. I do."

We sling on our backpacks once more, gaze to the mountainous horizon like pioneers or frontiersmen, and begin the trek. The romance of setting off into what appears like a dramatic Hollywood set is palpable—tropical rainforest, soaring mountains, rebel territory, even the sight of us all kitted out to look like irregular volunteers in the Spanish Civil War (that being Chiapas etiquette: heavy boots and black cargo pants, t-shirt, and well-worn baseball cap)—male and female dressed about the same. But actually it is about clothes that are appropriate for the rough terrain, not just rebel chic. OK, maybe the Zapatista paliacates tied around the neck do make one look pretty cool. The romance of the situation lasts about ten minutes before we are knee deep in swampy mud.

Moving forward is hard work, and when we emerge from the mud, it's the steep hill and the sun, which is moving higher into the clear blue sky. The heat is punishing.

This is not a "hike." We are not doing this for pleasure or even a challenge. We are doing it to get to Roberto Arenas and avoid the difficult military checkpoint/base on the sole access road to the community—a point where activists have been nailed before. As water workers, we do this march because it's part of the job of being a clandestine solidarity worker in autonomous rebel territory.

A couple of hours later, under the blistering sun, as the group slogs slowly up the mountainside, I become distracted—maybe mild delirium—by eavesdropping on the antics of the volunteers ahead of me.

Maria and Praxedis seem to have been discussing water valves, air-pressure, and the best concrete mixes for about two hours now. Sofia, the Italian; Tlaxlocaztla, the student; and Nebula, the squatter, walk together. The three women are buckled under the weight of their heavy backpacks, and helping each other along, while the boys, Omar and Josef, bicker every inch of the way over politics and ideology. I focus on Nebula and her slight figure as she battles on, clambering over fallen tree trunks, slipping over rocks, wading across little streams, and balancing upon treacherous tree trunk bridges over rivers. She may look like a crusty, ragamuffin pot-smoking layabout, but she is tough and up for it. I like her spirit. Sofia, on the other hand, is wise enough to know her limits. "I'm a fucking office worker! I can't go on! Stop!" she gasps, throwing her backpack down, dramatically, and falling on her back. Puffed red cheeks and chest heaving, it does seem a reasonable request. Everybody else is the worse for wear too—it's a good time for a food and water break.

People are relaxed and the mood is chill. The volunteers get into a discussion about their nom-de-guerre's. It became standard for volunteers on water projects to create a name for themselves for the duration of the project. This was ostensibly for security reasons, but it probably had more to do with paranoia. It was one paranoid activity that was fun, so nobody objected.

"So, are you called Sofia after your look-a-like, Sofia Loren?" asks Omar, somewhat flirtatiously.

"How flattering, Omar. No, my Sofia is short for Filosofia."

"I'm calling myself after Omar Little. Best gay role-model on television!"

Not everyone gets that one, as not a lot here watch US television, and it is well before *The Wire* becomes an international phenomenon.

"Who are you named after, Josef?" asks Nebula. "Stalin?"

"Go fuck yourself, hippy. What is Nebula? A flower?"

"Moron."

"I think Josef calls himself after his other hero," joins in Tlaxlocaztla. "Mengele!"

She and Nebula crack up, laughing together.

"You keep out if it, Loca," snaps Josef.

Those three have got off to a bad start, I notice.

"What about you, Tlaxlocaztla?" asks Maria. "Where did you get your name. Is it Aztec?"

"Well, kind of. My real name is, like, Maria-Teresa, you know, so they call me Terry and, as I prepared for my return to Mexico, I had a dream and in it my forefathers came to me and like, gave me this name. I felt like it was, you know, like, oh my God, being re-born again."

Tlaxlocaztla tells us she was carried up on foot over the border as a young child by her migrating parents. They left a small town in Guerrero and made it to Los Angeles. Despite the initial hardship, her parents thrived economically and the child grew up as a stereo-typical US suburban shopping-mall-kid speaking English as her first language and leaving behind all remnants of her native culture. Now, as an adult, she is returning to her roots, rediscovering her lost (or stolen) identity.

"OK, compañeros and compañeras, let's get going," says Praxedis. "We have a long way to go yet."

And the going is easy enough, along mountain top ridges and up and down none too challenging hills. It just takes a long time because the group is very slow. At one point, Praxedis, Maria, and I climb a hill and have to wait about half an hour for the others to catch up.

"You guys don't really want to get to work, do you? What you really want to do is camp out under the stars tonight, right?" chides Maria.

Yeah!

"Well sorry, that's not part of the program. Come on guys, we are running way late."

Josef proves an intriguing character. He arrived here through impeccable sources, and carried a stellar reputation from his years of activity in the European radical scene. There was the famous story of valiant defense of a squatted house in Warsaw, attacked late at night by a gang of neo-nazis and how he had played a key role in holding off the assailants and alerting the sleeping residents— children and old folks included—thereby saving the house, and securing the inhabitants' retreat. Such actions earned him a certain aura of antifa/autonome superstar. And then there is his intellectual guile: he has supposedly read (and understood) Marx's *Das Kapital* in three languages.

"Hey man, what's up?" I say, approaching him.

"Do you have a problem?" he replies with a distinct note of hostility.

"No, just wanna make sure your doing OK. I see you're getting some slagging there from the girls."

"That is because they are assholes."

OK, this guy is a real piece of work. I'm trying to act as conciliator, make bridges: it is proving more difficult than imagined.

Walking we ask questions.

"What brought you to Chiapas?"

"What does it matter? I am here now. I think this delegation is badly organized. I expected more committed people, not these jokers on-board."

All the people on the delegation arrived here, just like him, recommended by "movement" people we trust, with solid credentials that they would contribute productively.

"Give them a chance; you've only just met them."

"Liberal NGO do-gooders. I've met their types before. And lefty nationalists, even worse. Makes me puke."

"Quite frankly, Josef, I find that sectarian and closed-minded."

There is no talking to some people. I give up and walk ahead.

And now we have another problem—we are lost. It's taken more than nine hours so far and we are still wandering along the crest of the mountain that seems to just present itself with more crests, more hidden inclines, slopes, little valleys, but there's no decline down into the river basin in sight. We are on top of the mountain, but it keeps on stretching out, and I hadn't remembered it being this long before. Praxedis is confused too, and I fear we have completely lost our track and wandered in some perpendicular direction. It's getting into the late afternoon. The sun is setting, and images of some old horror movie like *Blair Witch* come to mind. We really might be horribly lost. Panic is gripping a little, but Maria, Praxedis, and I, supposedly the trail guides, keep it under our hats. I'm pretty sure we should have turned left at that huge boulder at the last ravine. But I don't fucking know! Fuck!

"Are we lost?" demands Josef. "You said six hours and we have already walked much more. This is appalling! I told you we should have discussed the logistics of this hike in a group meeting!"

Maria moves towards him, grimacing, as if to square off. They are caught in this cinematic moment facing each other, eye to eye, and neither blinks. The pair are a stark contrast. Josef is tall, lean and dressed head to foot in black, even his peaked hat. He sports a short grizzly beard and thick black glasses, his pale face locked in a permanent frown. Maria is small and petite, but I wouldn't underestimate the strength in that taut bow of a body. She wears colorful clothes made up of indigenous fabrics, and her tanned complexion, big brown eyes, and blond streaks in her auburn hair give her a glowing, *uber*-healthy look. They are two opposites.

"I am not in agreement," says Josef.

"You are perfectly entitled to your opinion, Josef," she says, "but what we need now is people to work together, not to just offer criticism. OK?"

"Very well," says Josef, stepping down.

Sofia intervenes, offering around the last of her water to each party. She should be wearing a blue helmet. A tense moment dissipates.

Maria takes off in front, with Praxedis and me in her wake.

"Damn, I'm getting pissed off having to deal with some of these arrogant assholes," she says quietly to Praxedis.

"We can send him back alone, if you want," he says, smiling somewhat cruelly.

"Yeah, it is definitely an option."

Of course it isn't. Joking aside, how do we deal with a character that is constantly imposing himself negatively and undermining the good spirit of things?

Meanwhile, I'm really hoping that we haven't wandered so far off course that we could find ourselves walking around the next corner into an army base or a hostile paramilitary community.

Nothing like being lost in the middle of nowhere to test one's endurance. Nerves are getting frayed and people are losing patience with each other.

"Let's turn back! This is crazy, we have to go back to Garrucha," says one.

"Are you crazy? Let's just set up camp somewhere for the night and continue in the morning," says another.

"No, let's split up. One group go north and one group go west."

"That's got to be the most ridiculous idea I have ever heard..."

Things are falling apart.

But lo-and-behold, we turn a corner and there it is, Roberto Arenas, a few kilometers away in the distance, snug by the riverbank at the bottom of the wide valley. We look down and know that our grueling journey's end is within sight. It takes no more than an hour to scamper down the mountain path. Suddenly the weight of the backpacks is lifted and we skip down, delighted with ourselves.

"Did you enjoy a pleasant day's hiking?" asks Praxedis, facetiously.

"Character-building march. Thanks a lot," says the Italian with a wry smile.

It is fully dark by the time we make the flat plain. We are stumbling around in the pitch-black forest now, the path invisible and our meager flashlights useless. But there is something very enchanting about emerging from the dense forest into the open space. The moon is rising over the mountain and the world is a translucent blue, mystical and pregnant with wonder. Hollywood set time once more, and at the end of a long journey, there is nothing more deserved than a good welcome—but, no, there is no one, the village is deserted, maybe sleeping.

We walk into the village fanned out like the Magnificent 7—except we are eight and, unlike the movie, we didn't save any unfortunate Mexicans with our heroic endeavor. We walked over a big fucking mountain, that's all.

"Hey guys, can I set up the camera and film this?" says Omar. "Can you all walk out of the forest again like that? *Very* cinematic..."

"Are you fucking crazy, man?" asks Nebula. Everybody cracks up laughing. Even Josef finds the idea amusing.

We arrive at the school building, our quarters, and find a youngster asleep with a crackling radio apparatus by his side. The Zapatista radioman is also meant to be the night guard, protecting the community, so not too impressed is he to be woken by no less than eight stomping caxlanes entering his rebel community in the dark of night. His pleading eyes ask us not to report him, and he runs off to wake Don Sisifo, *el jefe*. We assure him that all is well and he can rest easy; we wont report his transgressions.

"But why are you filming me with your camera?" he asks.

"Omar! Turn off the fucking camera," snaps Maria.

"Sorry, I just wanted to capture the moment..."

We are pleased with ourselves and, amidst much chatter and buffoonery, we start pitching our hammocks or making our beds out of children's school benches. Everybody is getting on well now and has found common ground. Illumined by flickering candlelight and hand-held flashlights, there's also what could be described as a flirty mood abounding among the chaos.

Sofia sets up her hammock quite deliberately next to Praxedis's bed. He gallantly offers to tie the hammock ropes around the high ceiling beam, and Sofia accepts the gesture, even though she is well able to do it herself.

"Thank you so much!" she says, briefly touching his arm, and gazing into his eyes a moment too long.

Praxedis blushes.

"Get a room you two," interjects Nebula, chortling.

She is undressing. The open school room offers no privacy but she has no concerns about false modesty.

"What are you staring at?" she demands of Omar, who is gazing intently at her chest.

"Haven't you seen a pair of breasts before?"

"Oh yeah, you probably haven't," she adds, somewhat nastily.

"Don't worry, honey, I have seen plenty of breasts and much more impressive than those. Actually, I am fascinated by your piercings."

Nebula has a heavy barbell piercing in one nipple, and a large silver ring through the other. Alongside the leaping tiger tattoo splayed across her chest, it all makes for quite an impressive display.

"We need some discipline here!"

This predictably enough, comes from Josef who is scowling in the corner, upset by all this lascivious, anti-revolutionary behavior.

"I think we need a sentry to do guard duty outside for a while," says Tlaxlocaxtla. "Step up, Comrade Josef!"

There is a gentle knock on the wall.

Don Sisifo appears out of the darkness somewhat sheepishly, "The group has arrived!"

"Yeah. Finally," says Maria. "And what happened to the compañeros who didn't meet us?"

Don Sisifo is not giving much away. "We are sorry. There was a problem."

"A problem here or a problem there?" asked Maria, pointing over the mountains.

"A little bit here, a little there," says Don Sisifo, ambiguously. "But now, is everything alright? Did you bring everything?"

"No, we left most of the equipment in Garrucha. We need horses. Can someone bring them over the mountain? Tomorrow?"

Don Sisifo looks troubled. "The compañeros there said it was OK?"

"Yes, of course."

"Yes, yes, I will see what can be done."

"And the extra picks," he adds, "did you bring them?"

Ah yes, the picks. Our backpacks are full of metal taps and pipes and valves and specialized tools but no, we forgot the picks again. Shit. So we are still a few picks short. Too bad. That means the volunteers won't be doing any digging. Maybe that is just as well.

Praxedis asks the all-important question: "How is the water, Don Sisifo?"

"Very good," he says. "Still flowing out of the pipe at the same rate as before."

That is great news.

And so, Don Sisifo heads back into the darkness again, bidding us a good night.

"And we left the battery-powered lamp in the school room so you can have a little light..."

I am slightly disappointed to hear of the advent of a battery-powered light in our room. I had been enjoying the primitive romance of the iridescent candlelight accompanying our previous stay here. But I suppose with eight campers lodging here now will need a little light to avoid psychological meltdown.

And finally, after a difficult day, we lay our heads down on bundled up sweaters, our makeshift pillows. I feel a bit sorry for the newcomers and the challenges ahead as they learn to deal with chaquistas and other nighttime irritants, but they do seem to have covered every inch of the room with anti-bug burning incense and showered their bodies liberally in smelly anti-mosquito spray. In the end, it's not the various chemicals and devices that drive the swarms of chaquistas and mosquitoes out of the cozy schoolroom, but the laughter and rumpus in the room—the chatty, infectious mirth of a group of people who have found a common spirit and shared gladness through haphazard endeavor and some degree of hardship. Bar one, of course.

"*Compañeros, silencio, por favor*," grumbles Josef from the darkest corner. "Time to sleep."

Cement Tanks And Tigers

I awake to the pitter-patter of little feet around the schoolroom. The children have all rushed over to see the new arrivals.

"And the ball?" asks a little boy named Jorge.

"The ball, the ball, the ball," they all start to chant in unison.

Fortunately for me—otherwise I would be on my way to San Cristobal before breakfast—I did indeed bring the football we promised, and I dig it out of my backpack. I brought a red and black one, like the Zapatista flag. And I brought one of those too, to hang in the schoolroom now, and later to give to the community.

Little Marisol appears and gives Maria a big embrace. Praxedis and I look at each other forlornly and shrug, nobody embracing us. Then Marisol, the sweety, comes around and gives us both a hearty hug.

Adelita arrives with a bundle of fresh, hot tortillas tied in a pretty pink napkin.

"Welcome back," she says, and indeed, it feels good to be back. It has been over a week since we left.

"How are things?" asks Maria.

"Good. The compas are very excited to move forward with the work. Although Alfredo is sick. Fever..."

Bad?

Yes.

That's not good. One of the water responsables down sick.

"And how is your mother, Doña Consuela?" asks Maria, being polite.

"Yes, she is sick in bed too."

"I'm sorry to hear it. When did all this sickness start?" Maria asks. "After the water arrived in the community?"

"No," says Adelita. "My mother is sick for a couple of weeks now, and Alfredo and some of the children became sick around the time you left. Before the people started using the new water."

"We will check it anyway," says Maria. The water supply... She's already gotten the test results for the first sample we sent to the lab, which indicated it was of excellent quality.

"*Bueno*, time for breakfast," announces Praxedis. He got up at dawn, made the fire, and prepared eggs and coffee for everyone.

"*Che bravo ragazzo!*" says the Italian, impressed.

Everyone heads over to the kitchen.

"Hang on, what's that?" asks Josef, as I step up on a bench to hang the flag over the doorway.

An EZLN flag, I say, "what is the problem?"

"It's a red star. I would prefer a black star. Or at least a black flag."

"Fine, great idea. We can have both. How about you make a big black flag with a big black star?"

Christ, this guy is a hassle.

All the men are gathered in the center of the community, ready to work, and keen to get at it. Introductions are made and everybody shakes hands. Timid, intrigued glances on both sides.

Maria steps up and outlines the next stage of the project and a plan of action for the next two weeks.

We are going to build a 13,000 liter reservoir tank here upon the solid concrete base that we finished at the end of the last stage. The cement floor is good—I am relieved; Praxedis and I did well. Tank construction will involve making a large wire frame, like a giant wrought-iron basket reinforced with chicken wire, and coating it with a multitude of layers of cement, layer after layer, inside and out, until it all binds, drying to form a concrete structure capable containing the water. It is a job that will take about a week, and will involve endless rounds of cement mixing and troweling. It is tricky work, and if cracks develop in the cement coat, which often do, it can destroy the tank's ability to withstand the water's pressure.

So the job is slow, boring, laborious, and needs to be closely monitored. Fortunately, this community is very motivated, morale is high, and everyone seems to enjoy each other's company. With Maria organizing the volunteers and Don Sisifo organizing the community, the work teams are formed and everyone is soon busy as a bee. By midday, we have the frame in place and all hands are busy tying it together with wire. Many hands indeed make light work. The mood is particularly happy now because we are working in the village so the hordes of children can hang around joining in and adding to the fun. Laughter and smiles predominate. Everybody is keen to get to know the new volunteers and they are thrilled to be on the receiving end of so much attention. Maria, Praxedis, and I are relieved to be out of the limelight at last.

"*Tigrio, tigrio!*"

A young man comes running up the hill in a state of great excitement, shouting away in Tzeltal. Suddenly, all the men drop their tools and start running off down the hill, whooping and shouting. Apparently a little wild jungle cat — a tigrio in local slang — has been spotted in somebody's back yard. Work, interrupted. Soon men with rifles appear all over the community it hot pursuit of the culprit who has being stalking the chickens.

Despite the exuberance of the hunt, the wild cat somehow escapes. An hour later, the men return, dejected. No dead tigrio. Back to the monotonous work.

"I don't think you should kill the cat," opines Josef.

"They carry away our chickens," explains Gordo. "And babies."

"Babies?!"

"Well I've never known a case of a baby being carried away here, but I *have* heard of it. It happened in another country."

"But still, you shouldn't kill the cat. It is a rare species."

Gordo is very clear. "Well, compa, if it kills our chickens, we must kill it."

We work late. The men mad into it, these people just don't stop. By 3 PM, the wire mesh frame, which resembles a zoo cage, is done. A picturesque cover resembling a circus tent is hoisted above our heads to keep rain and sun off the construction site and it all feels quite vaudeville.

We have scheduled a group meeting for the afternoon. Returning from the river, the volunteers are exuberant and laughter rings out.

"Damn, it's like a tropical riverside beach resort down there!"

"Yep, Zapatista Springs, an exotic delight for all you revolutionary tourists!" mocks Praxedis. "We should charge you for the privilege of coming to work here."

"That is a good idea," muses Maria. "Reality vacations."

"Cheap holidays in other people's misery," says Josef, disgusted at the notion.

Later, everyone squeezes in around the rough kitchen table while Praxedis and I prepare food, and the group meeting is called into session.

Maria gives a rundown of the usual procedure for volunteers in communities, the rules and regulations. Fairly basic: don't wander off into the hills alone (it's dangerous, and one could run into the military or paramilitaries), don't give individual people money (creates dependencies), and don't make promises you won't follow up on. Finally, Maria requests that people remember they are guests in the village and respect the *usos y costumbres* of the local people.

"Even if they are wrong?"

"Excuse me?" says Maria, with that kind of scary, don't-fuck-with-me tone.

"Like killing endangered cats," says Josef. "Here is a case where *usos* and *costumbres* go against the great common good, and the right of these beautiful animals to exist."

This guy has a lot of work to do on his internalized oppressions, I'm thinking.

Internalized oppression in the field of international solidarity is manifested when privileged activists from the north impose their group's belief system and values over the people they encounter in the south. This "pathology of privilege" is often expressed in either super-radical or liberal-individualist positions taken by activists coming from radical milieu bubbles in the US or Europe (or wealthy southern metropolitan nodes).

"Dude, it is a valid point, but I recommend that you leave your presumptions behind," says Maria, "and try listening for a moment. De-colonize yourself, comrade!"

This is an on-going debate that will impact the group throughout their stay. I understand it as a dialectic interaction between a militant ideologue and a rational pragmatist—or the absolutism of Josef and the relativism of Maria. Josef understands the world through the prism of his theoretical reading and understanding of anarcho-syndicalism and Marxism, while Maria interprets things through her ethical sense of justice and righteousness, and always prioritizes the perspective of the marginalized—in this case, the indigenous Zapatista.

The discussion swings towards more immediate matters at hand.

Omar and Tlaxlocaztla want to know if it is alright to record the proceedings and conduct interviews with the compañeros.

Maria explains that the community have given permission for the work to be recorded, but are uncertain about the interviews—they want to know what the line of investigation will be and what will be done with that information. They asked for Tlaxlocaztla and Omar to make a presentation of their intentions before the community assembly.

Tlaxlocaztla makes the further request to stay with a family.

"It important for my investigations to get insight into the day-to-day life of the indigenous," she explains. "No offense, you guys are all pretty awesome and I like hanging with the group, but I'd prefer to be with my *paisanos,* fellow Mexicans."

Part of the process of rediscovering her Mexican identity involves prioritizing all things Mexican, and rejecting all that she grew up with in the US. A laudable quest, which she is undertaking with some zeal. She has discarded her heavy LA accent in favor of a halting Spanglish, or English with a heavy Mexican accent, and often forgets words in English. She has replaced her groovy, emo-style clothes with a traditional indigenous *huipil* and leather sandals, which she bought in the market in San Cristobal. Her hair, which she had previously worn loose with bangs is now in braids, American-Indian style.

"Terry does Pocahontas," teases Nebula.

Tlaxlocaztla is fuming at this joke. "That is totally racist! You don't understand! I have lived my whole life as someone else, and finally I am re-discovering the real me. Why are you, like, fucking with me?"

"Relax tiger, I am only kidding. I think it's cool what you are doing, but damn, you got to see the funny side of it. You were totally Terry from the hood a few days ago and now you are like fucking Tlaxlocaztla the noble Nahua *pipiltin!*"

"Yo fuck you, bitch," snaps Tlaxlocaztla, reverting back to a more familiar street cholo tone.

"To go back to the original request," intervenes Maria, "how about you come with me to talk to Don Sisifo about staying with a family. I am sure they would be into it."

The meeting then moves on to other issues on the agenda.

"Hey hey hey, what are you doing?!" interrupts Josef, addressing Praxedis who is busy disinfecting a jug of water for use tomorrow.

"What's up man?"

"I don't want iodine in my water. It's toxic. That stuff is like poison! It is as carcinogenic as cellphones!"

"Sorry dude, but I'm not willing to take a chance. This water is not fit to be drunk untreated," says Praxedis. "What do you propose?"

"I'll drink my own boiled water," says Josef.

"OK dude, no one is gonna force you drink anything you don't want to," says Maria. "But the local water is contaminated and dangerous—that is why we are here. It is not enough to just boil it, it needs to be disinfected, man."

"I'll take my chances."

"Alright, but anybody who gets sick on the water team is going back to San Cris. First bus at dawn outta here. We don't have time or space for non-productive volunteers."

I don't think she means it. Volunteers always get sick on water projects and we always look after them, so I think she is just taking the piss, or trying to rile him up. Part of the ongoing head-butting of two different characters, two distinct ways of looking upon things. For outside parties like myself, not in the middle of the squabbling, it is intriguing to observe. Maria's authority is derived from her experience and the sheer longitude of her presence here, and Josef bases his righteousness on the certainty of principles. Both are 100% down with the struggle, but see it in completely different terms. The Maria/Josef dialectical.

Like many group meetings, this one could go on all night, but we have to work early tomorrow. We end up by organizing work schedules and shifts, like who will do the cooking and cleaning on each day.

The day ends with a group smoke outside the schoolroom under the starry sky and, despite the various intrigues, we conclude that all is well.

I wake at 6 AM and feel a quiet optimism. Praxedis and the Italian have been up since 5 preparing breakfast: group coffee, eggs, and a few cigarettes. Those who didn't smoke before this trip are, sadly, now smoking. Except Maria...she remains hardcore.

Today we begin mixing cement and applying the paste to the frame. The work is coming along rapidly as we finish a primary coat of the whole tank in one day. Six teams work on pasting, two or three sift the sand and mix the cement, and, as the sun shines, we advance solidly. By early afternoon we have all enjoyed ourselves during the construction of the first wall. Work is not work when it rushes along, and having good food, long breaks, and good company makes us all happy campers.

I notice that socializing between the caxlanes and the adult community members remains somewhat strained. There is of course the problem of language as most everyone is speaking Spanish as a second language, some with very rudimentary Spanish at that, and some speak only Tzeltal. So either the volunteers horse around with the children, or else they work. The community's adults remain exceedingly shy and wary of the newcomers, and they pretty much ignore me, Maria, and Praxedis, the familiar ones. I'm not sure why this distance remains. It is true that the mood and social dynamic is unique in each community where we undertake water projects, but, as a general rule, the further you get from the towns and the deeper into the jungle, the greater the bridge to cross, in terms of everyday socializing and relationship building. And the less present the women are in everyday social life.

"What do you think, Praxedis?" I ask on the side. "Is there a strange vibe between the group and the community?"

"No, I don't think so. They are all just shy. It will pass."

So the awkwardness between the volunteers and the community is probably not just due to the general isolation of this place or the fact that the community is not used to chit-chat with strangers or that we are the first caxlanes ever to come here. There's also the fact that we are a pretty extraordinary bunch of caxlanes. Nebula faces a series of bemused questions pertaining to her dreadlocks, dyed hair, tattoos, and piercings—don't think these people have ever seen anything like her in their lives. Or Omar, whose face seems to be pasted to that camera that he rarely puts down—probably the only Arab in the whole Lacandon Jungle—and gay, to boot! And Sofia, even in her muddy, cement-crusted clothes, looks like she just stepped off a Milan catwalk, exuding movie-star glamor even when she wields a shovel.

But mostly the questions directed to the newcomers concern the cost of their boots, how much it is for a plane ticket to Mexico, and the possibility for a Mexican peasant to work without papers in the newcomer's home country.

The visitors are having a distinct difficulty relating to the mountain people and their world. Josef is getting particularity frustrated as he asks overtly political questions and gets silence in return.

"What do you think of Marcos's last communiqué about the Basque struggle?" he asks.

Nobody here in this village has read the last communiqué of Sub Marcos about the Basque struggle because they have little notion of these things. (And who can read anyhow?) It is not just that they are isolated geographically; their concerns are local and immediate and the poetic writings of Marcos on behalf of the EZLN have little or no relevance to their daily lives here. It is a strange anomaly to be an outsider or caxlan journeying to and from the Lacandon Jungle and being the carrier of the news about what the Zapatistas are doing or saying on a national or international level. These outlying communities usually have heard nothing of Marcos or the Clandestine Committee's latest communiqués and pronouncements. There is a strange disjunction between the central Zapatista headquarters, the caracoles, and then the communities on the periphery. The distance is not just geographic, mediated by difficult nodes of communication, but due mostly to the

fact that the majority of the EZLN communiqués are directed out-
ward, while the concerns of the people here are immediate, local.

As Maria and Praxedis move about doing other work, I am left
"in charge," or better say, as point person for the work team on the
tank. I am somewhat of an unassuming foreman, preferring to let
the workers do it at their own pace and skill, rather then hovering
over them, telling them how to do everything. It is all a bit messy,
but the mood is lively and the people animated, so I think it is all
going well. We are moving ahead on the second coat at a steady
pace. Another layer of creamy cement is applied upon what is now
a solid concrete structure and when it has dried sufficiently, we
wash down the tank sides with water from the pipe. It's slow work,
poco a poco, but as ever, we are happy workers. I begin to notice a
subtle contrast in how the teams work. The volunteers are gung-
ho and begin working on their own individual initiative, only asking me occasional questions pertaining to the cement mix or what
part of the wall to work on. The compas on the other hand, pretty
much ignore me, don't take individual initiative, but always work
collectively. They look to Don Sisifo for direction. Don Sisifo is

most definitely the foreman of the compas; he organizes them into work-groups and tells them what to do. Here I am "point-man," and rather than leading, I am merely moving to the side and allowing Don Sisifo to step up and organize it all. The way they replicate old forms of hierarchy with their division of labor, I don't know any other model that could work effectively at this point.

But, individually or collectively, these people work hard. Even Maria, back from scoping out the distribution system in the village, is happy with the pace. "Well done, Ramon," she says. I blush. Me? I didn't do anything!

After three days labor, we have the first layer of the tank complete. It's more like porridge than perfect cement and it kind of butters on with the trowels. So while teams mix the cement in little pools—the heavy work—about half a dozen people trowel the mix on the frame. Working in each other's shadow, we thrive—we are looking at something that resembles a tank. People are pleased with the tempo of the work and the feeling of moving forward.

It's time to visit the sick. Maria goes around to Adelita's house to see Doña Consuela, armed with some flowers and fruit, and Praxedis and I head over to Alfredo's house on the edge of the community. His house is as a basic as anybody else's here, with its earthen floor, wooden walls, and leaky roof, but his bedroom is a separate structure off to the side. It is dark and depressing, with a few sticks of furniture, a bundle of clothing, and little else. It is eerily reminiscent of very old portraits of Irish rural homes during the famine in the 1840s. Worse still, is the visage of the stricken Alfredo, laid up on his bare board bed with a couple of well-worn blankets. He looks pale and drawn, with beads of sweat rolling down his forehead. He has a raging fever, constant diarrhea, and complains of an intense headache, fatigue, and chills. It seems like a pretty extreme case of Salmonella or Typhoid. His wife Victoria attends to him, keeping him well hydrated. He is taking nothing except some herbal remedy brought by Don Job, the village health responsable and a few aspirins. I'm thinking he needs serious medical attention, but what can be done when the nearest clinic and doctor is hours away in Ocosingo? There is an autonomous clinic operating in Garrucha, but it is almost equidistant to the state-run hospital in Ocosingo, and the road to get there is rougher.

"How are you feeling, compa?" asks Praxedis.

"Not good, compa," replies Alfredo.

We feel useless and powerless. Maybe he needs antibiotics and not just the apple we brought, but without a diagnosis what can we do? We are amateur plumbers not amateur doctors.

Alfredo turns over and clearly wishes to be left alone. Though it does nothing for her husband, Doña Victoria appreciates the apple—clearly a commodity rarely seen in this neck of the woods. She places it on a little altar near the bed, graced by an image of the Virgin of Guadalupe and photos of Emiliano Zapata and Sub-comandante Marcos. We wish Alfredo well and say we will check in tomorrow.

"How is Doña Consuela?" we ask Maria when we regroup back at the schoolroom.

"Not good," she says. "She is flat out and it is very worrying. Adelita and Don Job are going to take her to the clinic on the bus tomorrow."

"Shit. Should we help with the transport costs?"

"I already did."

We have organized the kitchen to accommodate eight of us. It is now well stocked, two people each day are designated to look after food preparation, cooking, cleaning, and making sure there is a constant supply of potable water. We now have many cooks with fresh supplies and the time to make good food. Everything is going smoothly, and people step up to take responsibility for the various tasks—cutting firewood, setting the fire, washing up, etc. Not because somebody tells them to do so, but because there is a healthy spirit of mutual aid, and chores become a shared pleasure. It is a very different environment from when only Praxedis and I were here, and, after long hard days of work, we would generally just drag ourselves to the kitchen to prepare the quickest, easiest supper before collapsing back in the schoolroom for the night.

The following day, it's my turn for kitchen duty and I'm teamed up with Omar—something I've been looking forward to because he seems a pretty interesting guy. I get to the kitchen first and start cutting wood and preparing the fire. Omar wanders in, camera stuck to his face.

"Oh come on, Omar, no camera. It's too early."

"But the light is wonderful, the beams of the rising sun coming through the kitchen wall and the fire dancing on your face!... Please let me film you!

I submit on one condition: he only records me with my face covered. Security, you understand.

Yes, yes of course.

It has nothing to do with security, I couldn't give a rat's ass if he shoots or not, I'm just camera shy. Hate them.

So I don a Zapatista *pasamontana*—a balaclava—and since I'm about to start cooking, I put on the apron that Praxedis so thoughtfully packed. Omar gets his beautiful shot of the translucent light and the flames pirouetting and there's me in a balaclava and a pink apron, stirring eggs.

"What kind of movie you making, Omar? Some kind of slapstick comedy?"

"No, no, no," he says quite earnestly. "I want to film the everyday vitality of the Zapatista autonomous revolution in action. It's the moments in-between that I want to capture. Not the obvious stuff, but the little things in-between that capture an essence."

"OK, want to film me cutting garlic?"

"Perfect darling. Can you pout a little more while doing it?"

Sure, but you won't see much behind the balaclava.

"No, that is what I'm after," he jokes, sarcastically, "the lascivious pouting behind the mask. Isn't it absolute Zapatismo?!"

He is a funny guy, this Omar. I ask him how he ended up here.

Like many, it came through reading Marcos's early communiqués, dripping with wit and wisdom.

"I was on-location in Northern Africa, working on some photo shoot. Someone had a book of Marcos's writings and I was hooked. The whole 'Marcos is a gay waiter in San Francisco' kind of discourse, very inclusive. Reading Marcos in Tangier, then."[1]

"Maybe that should be the working title of my movie," he muses.

He returned to Brighton where he was studying for an MA in film, and got active in a solidarity group.

"So why the Zapatistas and not some other social movement?" I inquire.

---

1. Marcos is gay in San Francisco, black in South Africa, an Asian in Europe, a Chicano is San Ysidro, an anarchist in Spain, a Palestinian in Israel, a Mayan Indian in the streets of San Cristobal, etc.

"I suppose I was enamored by the freshness of Zapatismo, the idea of fighting in order not to take power, their practice of leading by obeying, a rebel movement that spoke so eloquently. Everything for everybody, nothing for ourselves. Walking, we ask questions. These kinds of slogans, such beautiful ideas."

As an Arab, did Zapatismo strike a chord?

"Absolutely. In the sense that Zapatismo doesn't come from the core centers, like Europe or North America, it comes from the peripheries, and talks to other peripheries like, say, the Berber struggle, bypassing the concentrations of power and wealth. It is an anti-systemic movement, transnational, and if only more people in the Arab world got to know about Zapatismo, I think it would have a huge effect."

The student, Tlax, walks in during Omar's eloquent presentation. "Someone here has studied their Wallerstein. Nice!"

Then she turns to me. I'm still done up somewhat theatrically in balaclava and apron. "Oh sorry, I didn't mean to disrupt the burlesque show. Want to borrow my heels?"

"Can't a man cook a few eggs in peace?!"

Campo cooking is about the balance between keeping the fire going steadily and not burning everything in the process. Cooking under difficult conditions. But one can't really fuck up too much with a pan full of scrambled eggs on one side and a pot full of beans on the other. The hungry workers will devour whatever is put in front of them, once there's tons of garlic in it.

"Mmmm, smells good," says Tlax.

"How are things in the house?" I ask her.

She is staying at Gordo's house, with his wife Regina and their four kids.

"It's great. They are a really awesome family. Regina rocks. Only they don't eat much of anything except tortillas and beans. I'm starving all the time. Hmm, those eggs look good."

Meanwhile, back on the building site, things are racing along as Maria, back at the reins, has everyone fired up. The walls are almost complete and now we are turning to the roof. We assemble basic, rough scaffolding. The campesinos are handy carpenters. With the community's only chainsaw they fashion rough planks of wood from various fallen trees scattered around the place. Soon we have a sturdy scaffold and begin the delicate work of getting buckets of cement up there to plaster the dome-like metal frame. The younger compañeros love this part of the work—the more difficult and dangerous the better—and nothing fills them with more glee than the sight of one of their number slipping on the scaffold or dropping a dollop of cement on the unfortunate below them.

By Saturday afternoon we have almost completed the structure. It's solid and impressive. To celebrate, we knock off earlier than usual in order to hike to the best part of the river for a wash and a swim. Some kids lead us through the thick forest for about fifteen minutes and we emerge at a little forest bower beside the Jataté. There is a flat, sandy bank here that gives the sense of a pretty beach. "Lacandon Cancun!" we name it with delight. The weekend starts here, woah!

People strip down to their underwear and jump in. The pristine natural surrounding would encourage somewhat hippy behavior, like going in naked, but protocol forbids that. Caxlanes are requested to maintain a little modesty in the Zapatista communities, and in any indigenous community, in fact. The reason given is modesty is part of the indigenous culture. Other people, especially activists from Spain or Northern Europe with more familiarity with nakedness, would argue that that is a moral and social more imposed by the conquesting Catholic church, but that is not an argument anyone is going to make now. The truth on the ground is that the women from the communities generally bathe topless, but with some kind of slip. The men wear their underpants, but there is often a special men's place where they bathe naked. There is also a special women and children only spot, but I've no idea what goes on there.

"Wanton abandonment," Maria assures me. "Just wild."

Josef, as usual, is complaining.

"Man, this is completely fucking retarded, having to wear my boxers into the water," he bemoans.

"Yo, could you put your t-shirt back on too, please," jokes Tlaxlocaztla. "Your ugly, white-ass bony chest is making me retch."

The river is green and subdued. A pig languishes nearby. A little boy joins us and fishes with an old rusty hook on the end of a piece of string. Two youths are fishing out further, water up to their waists. We ask them have they caught much.

Nada! Nothing.

How big are the fish here?

They reply with a hand measurement. About the size of a goldfish, oh dear.

Sofia is concerned. Her NGO-mindset kicks in.

"It would be so easy to improve the diet of the people here, with just a couple of development projects."

"Such as?" asks Maria.

"I mean for instance here, with a little help, the community could start a fish farm, start producing bigger, more nutritious fish. If it took off, they could even eventually make a little money selling the product."

"I think the communities are always interested in ideas for development. Can your NGO in Italy support a project?"

"I could propose it."

"You would have to go through the junta in La Garrucha."

"Oh yeah. We would respect the appropriate procedures of course."

"This is such bullshit," Josef offers, making his presence known.

"Why?"

"It's more of this development model bullshit of the UN or the World Bank. Like greater production is the key to prosperity and progress. The underlying principle is an economic one, and thus, towards a western universality."

"No," argues Sofia, "it is more along the lines of 'Give them fish they will eat for a day, teach them to fish and they will eat all their lives.' Except in this case because of the apparent lack of fish there is a little industry involved. It is sustainable, an eco-friendly development."

"No, that's even worse. First of all, it's imposing a technology like fish farming, which is not indigenous to the region or part of the people's customs. Secondly, it's the whole model of imposing things on people. Ready-made solutions that might have worked in Italy or somewhere, but there is no reason to think it would work here."

"It's the people's decision themselves if they want the development project, not yours and your ideology," this from Maria.

"You propose a fish farm to the community, of course they would except it. What have they got to lose? But you are not offering real alternatives. Just what your little tunnel vision NGO has to offer."

"The Zapatistas would say they don't want a fish farm, they want the river and the forest too!" says Praxedis.

"Yeah, to leave it as it is," says Josef. "They don't want any Italian NGOs coming in here and turning their indigenous society into a little market economy."

"That is not what I am proposing," says Sofia, well pissed off with Josef. "I'm just making a suggestion on how to improve their diet."

"They existed just fine without your suggestions for a long time," says Josef. "NGOs are always trying to make things better for people who don't need their intervention."

There is a lot of validity to his arguments, but his manner of arguing drives most people to wanting to throttle him.

"I don't think the community would agree with you there," says Maria. "Let's see what they have to say on the issue."

The compañeros have invited us to play basketball on their grassy, stony makeshift court. Necessity is the mother of invention and somehow they have managed to create a functioning basketball court out of nothing.

The compas and the water team have a grand time playing basketball, and at half time, as everyone rests, Maria brings up the fish proposal.

After discussing it in Tzeltal a while with the others, Don Sisifo, as ever, answers on behalf of the rest. "Yes, of course we would welcome such a project. We would welcome any project you would offer. We are thankful for your ideas."

I feel like I've seen way too many failed projects in my couple of years presence in the region to get too excited about the prospect. From rabbit rearing to electricity producing water turbines to smokeless stoves, many projects that simply didn't work out have come and gone. But I think the Zapatistas and the people in the communities have a pragmatic outlook on such endeavors: it's worth a try. Or sometimes their attitude seems more along the lines of not looking a gift horse in the mouth—if someone offers, take it.

Such discussions leave me weary. In many ways I would echo Josef's argument that it would be better if solutions came from within instead of without, but people are entrenched in their own unwieldy position. Instead of engaging with it, I retreat from the group and read under a tree. Sometimes the constant socializing is difficult to deal with. Sleeping aside, one is always surrounded by a bunch of people and engaging communally. Hell is other people. Eventually, at least for me, socializing becomes a chore, an endeavor to get through, and anti-social habits emerge. However selfish and self-absorbed that it may seem in the context of this collectively-premised work, if the opportunity arises, I will disappear to the river to read.

I like the serenity of the riverbank where we bathe. The river is wide at this point, and the flow powerful. Fallen tree trunks litter its passage like languishing giants. On the other side of the river, the hills climb up, dense with jungle vegetation. All is silent apart from the great flow of water and the far-distant roar of thunder somewhere deep in the jungle. The wind picks up suddenly and catches the lush riverside ferns, giving way to a soft crescendo of willowy leaves blowing. I put pen to paper and write.

Reflecting upon the troubling group dynamics, I think the on-going tension between Maria and Josef is particularly worrisome. Josef is very attached to his beliefs and is completely assured as to the righteousness of his arguments. Maria is less ideologically minded, but is, I suspect, a little ego-driven and wants to be seen to be proven correct. She likes to be in charge and expects people on the project to respect her hard-earned authority in the field. Josef recognizes no authority but reason, and asserts his logic irrespective of other people's thoughts or feelings or knowledge. Social niceties are sentimental notions, and are alien to him. But his ideological staunchness is matched by her innate competitiveness, and as they constantly butt heads, it is somewhat fascinating to speculate on how it will pan out. Something has to give.

As ever, my introspective reveries are short lived, I'm now surrounded by a gaggle of inquisitive children, demanding my attention. A particularly endearing four-year-old called Cristina swings from my neck. Cristina, the girl who is always singing about strawberries despite the fact she has never seen one. I put the book down—who can resist such sweetness?

Sunday is a day of rest, and the community spends most of the day cloistered in the little structure beside the basketball court that serves as a church. Tzeltal religion is a syncretic mixture of Catholicism—introduced by Spanish colonialists—and traditional Mayan religion. If you peek in, you will see the men one side and the women on the other, with shawls draped over their bowed heads, and the children wandering free. The elderly are given privileged position at the head of the assembly. A designated catechist leads the service and he reads parts of the bible while the others reflect upon the words. The women are led by a *magrina* (the female holder of ceremonial office). Despite the pious etiquette of the catechists, the ritual is conducted in an informal and very social manner. Later, people gather in little groups in which one person will read from the bible, in Tzeltal, and the group (separated by gender) will discuss the word of the Lord. It is very much following the gospel of the preferential option of the poor, liberation theology.

We caxlanes, a bunch of atheistic heathens and unrepentant sinners, loll around lazy and content this sunny Sunday—a day of sloth, not rest. It has only been a week since we departed San Cristobal but we have done more physical work than most of us will do all year.

More out of boredom than a heretical desire to break religious taboos, we decide to relocate to the building site in the afternoon, and begin some undemanding work on a roof frame for the tank. So first we construct a rough wooden tower, and then cut the wire frame into triangle shapes to be tied into place as a mould for the cement. Intricate work.

In the late afternoon, Don Job, one of the older community members, comes down to join us. He is impressed by our commitment but nevertheless chides us gently.

"Sunday is God's day, you should be resting," he tells us. "Be good to yourselves, rest."

"Most of us never work, not on Sundays, not on any day, at least not like this," says the Italian Sofia, speckled in cement, a trowel in hand, laughing. "What do you think of sitting in front of a computer for eight hours a day, five days a week, Don Job?"

"Sounds like being locked up in jail," he says. "I would not like that."

"Yes, that is what it feels like," she agrees.

"Me, I like to be out in the jungle or on a mountainside

working on my milpa, just myself and nature, maybe with one of my sons for a little company," says Don Job waxing lyrical. "For sure it's hard work, planting corn, but at least I don't have a *patron* telling me what to do. For a while I worked on the coffee plantations down on the lowlands—what we call *tierra caliente*, hot country—and how we suffered there, with the manager always mistreating us! And the heat! No, never again. I prefer just to have my cornfield and feed my family. But the youth all want to go away, work up north. They say one can earn a lot of money."

Don Job is a grandfather of indeterminate age. He could be fifty-five or sixty-five, I can't tell, and it feels impolite to ask. Aside from being a subsistence farmer who successfully raised ten children ("ten Zapatistas," he says proudly), he is also the community health responsable, meaning in the absence of formal medical services in the community, he has accrued a store of medical knowledge using traditional herbal practices. When he can, he attends health courses over in the caracol in La Garrucha, where outside doctors and health workers impart more formal medical knowledge, and dispense some basic vaccines and drugs for community use.

"How is Doña Consuela getting on?" we ask, inquiring after Adelita's sick mother.

"*Mas o menos*," he says. "So-so. We brought her to the hospital in Ocosingo yesterday. She is very sick. Her daughter is staying with her."

"By the way," he says, nonchalantly, "I noticed water spurting out of the pipe near the river."

Praxedis and I react like a fire brigade unit, already running in the direction of the river before Don Job has finished the sentence. The others laugh.

"Wait for us!" Maria shouts out. "Don't worry, it is not going anywhere soon..."

In a craggy ravine by the side of the river, someone has pulled a section of pipe out of the trench, and sure enough, from a sizable hole the water is exiting with remarkable pressure, like a mini street-hydrant. From the gnawing marks around the hole we can ascertain that a mole has eaten through the hard plastic.

We can replace this section of the tube—that is no problem— but what can be done with the outstanding problem of the pipe-chewing moles? Potentially disastrous, if all his mates get a similar idea. The area is crawling with moles.

Other compañeros arrive on the scene of the crime and gather around. Don Job is in conference with some of his sons.

"We can shoot the mole," he suggests.

(Shhh! Don't let Josef hear you!)

But what if there are lots of moles?

Praxedis suggests lining the pipes with hot chile salsa along this section—moles apparently have no appetite for hot salsa.

"Gringo moles!" jokes Praxedis and everybody cracks up laughing. Maria and I don't find this particularly amusing. But more importantly what can be done about this seemingly significant mole problem?

"Today is Sunday," says Don Job. "We will deal with it tomorrow."

Everyone agrees.

We have a bad start to our Monday morning. The outside layer of cement on the frame has dried over the weekend and, to our disappointment, is cracked and no good. Basically it appears to have been a hack job and now it's fissuring off the metal frame. The group of youths had overseen the job a little too hastily and with a little too much horseplay. What can you expect from a group of excited school kids fooling around? Of course they aren't really children—they are responsible male community members, some with wives and children, and all with their own plots of corn to oversee and the community responsibilities that come with being an adult—but they are also a bunch of teenagers, aged fifteen to nineteen, and they haven't had much of a childhood. Kids become adults here and often there is no in-between. Nonetheless, the spirit of youth manifests itself in the chaotic and rebellious joy of making play of work.

So it was my fault as "foreman," or responsable, that I didn't impose discipline. I was enjoying the youthful exuberance too much. And now I must cede my authority to Maria. She assumes the reins with greater rigor.

"Why is the tank cracked?" she asks sternly. "Was it the cement mix or the lack of water?"

We surmise it must have been the suffocating heat of last week, and that we didn't apply enough water. We can't take any chances, so it all has to come off, the whole coat. A senior team, comprised of Don Sisifo and the older members of the community, is assembled to make sure there is no fooling around this time.

It disappoints me a little: my method of overseeing the work last week was premised on the idea that people could and can do it on their own, that they would take sufficient responsibility because it's not some alienating piece of work, but part of their own community development. Somewhat idealistically, or naively, I let the young people at it, trusting they would do a good job, embracing their own "autonomy." Instead the youngsters did shabby work. Maria, by contrast, is overseeing the work closely and making sure everyone does it right—basically ordering people what to do, like a perpetuation of old modes of labor and authority.

Or perhaps I am analyzing it too harshly: Sure, I made a bad call and, sure, Maria's more authoritarian methods get better results, but also it really was just the extraordinary heat of the sun.

It takes all morning chipping away to remove the first layer of cracked cement. With hammer and chisel, we tear it down, lamenting the wasted work. It represents a whole day's labor for

six people. That's about $1,000 worth of man-hours in the USA, but here in the jungle it's just time lost, and a little cement—it doesn't really matter too much. Josef is distinguishing himself in this work—he has knocked half the tank wall off now in his verve to make everything right.

We re-do the whole surface in record time, but taking great care with the mix and the application.

"More water! Mix in lots of water, lots of water," Maria repeats, like a mantra. With brushes we apply layer after layer of cement, now the consistency of milk. Everyone is sweating buckets as they trowel and mix cement. The day is suffocatingly hot, but by the end of it, it's looking good.

And now for the roof. It is to look like a mosque, round and majestic, "like Al Aqsa," as Omar says. We wire up the wooden roof frame and throw on cement, everybody participating, laboring together. Once again we have been working from morning to evening, and it is a relief to call it a day.

40 Degrees in a Simmering Cauldron

The worst stage of the work is cementing inside the tank when the roof is on, and only a little hatch exists for air and light to come in. Meanwhile, the workers are inside the tank plastering on more layers of cement.

We are blessed with rain clouds and a cool wind today, like an Irish summer's day. Work on the inside will be a degree or two more tolerable.

We work in small teams of three. Each person climbs into the tank via the small entrance hole. It's like a death chamber inside, a tomb. All life is suspended in there: it's still and dark and claustrophobic, and the air is heavy, laden with cement particles. The tank's an assault of cement; it's like being in a city, as opposed to the feral jungle where we are. It's gruesome, tomb-like work. Most can only bear half an hour of it before climbing out again, gasping for fresh air. Here, however, Josef shines, and perseveres inside the tomb long after everyone else has bolted. He and Don Sisifo find common ground within the simmering cauldron of abrasive vapors.

To seal the inside of the tank, we need to apply a thick concrete coat to the walls and ceiling. But the inside surface needs to be even more flush than the outside wall, so it has to be worked in closely with a trowel, over and over. Then with spatchel or brush, a very fine going-over is applied, to really seal the inside of the tank.

The boys who made a mess of the exterior coat volunteer to work inside the tank with Sisifo and Josef, as a kind of penance, or just because they are good spirited and generous. I don't envy them as the day draws out and the heat inside the hellish chamber soars and the cloud of cement particles inside thickens, making the environment increasingly toxic and dangerous. But it must be done.

Meanwhile, the more fortunate workers outside enjoy the cool day and remain busy applying light layers of cement to the outer wall and constructing stone walls to protect the taps and fittings. Here I come into my element: I enjoy hand-crafting stone walls... Ireland is renowned for its abundance of little stone walls that snake across the landscape, especially in the west. So maybe it is in the blood, and I'm happy as a pig in shite making rough walls to protect the tank fittings, the entrance, and the exit tubes. I employ the children to collect stones for me, a job they undertake with enthusiasm.

"Typical imperialist, exploiting child labor," teases Praxedis.

The other volunteers make heavy cement lids to cover the tank and taps. The lids are heavy and burdensome, reinforced with rebar, and topped with wire handles. As they are laid out in the sun to dry, it is apparent that somebody has engraved their tag prominently on the drying cement:

"xJosefx."

"Well, who could have done that?" muses Omar, taking a photograph.

"Some pompous European with a messed-up idea of respecting the usos y costumbres of the community," says Maria, erasing the graffiti. In its place, she inscribes:

"Zapatista Spring, Roberto Arenas" and the day's date.

A team is dispatched to fix the mole-eaten tube by the river. Praxedis and Sofia, now inseparable, carry up the necessary tools, while Nebula and I go fetch some red-hot chili pepper from the kitchen. Our thinking is that trying out that method may be less hassle than having some rifle-toting hunters lingering around the trench all night waiting for mole intruders.

We cut the mole-chewed tube, and the pressure of the water flowing out of the ruptured tube is mighty, which is a very good sign. It is hard work inserting the plastic connector and we wrestle to get it in. All four of us, pushing and shoving, get soaked and covered in mud and fall over each other. Howling with laughter, it's a bit of a plumbing orgy. Eventually we get it in; the tube is fixed and the water is flowing inside the pipe again. We rub thick dollops of hot pepper over this section of tubing and hope that does the job to keep off the moles. If that doesn't work, I guess we'll have to call in the firing squad.

The day ends late. We are all in chirpy mood and the air is light with giggles. Strange and wonderful events are occurring on the water project. First, there is the predictable romance blossoming between the handsome Prince of Water Workers and the glamorous Italian NGO operative and philosopher—international solidarity royalty as such—which by now would have been consummated if the two weren't so hopelessly timid about it. And then there is the more unlikely coupling of Josef and Don Sisifo who have become thick as thieves, with Josef trailing around in Sisifo's wake, the two laboring together and sharing a strange esoteric wit that manifests itself in a sudden burst of gruff joviality. It is strange to see Don Sisifo laughing, something we have not seen so far; his usually somber, deeply-wrinkled face becomes filled with unbridled joy, so much so that it looks like it might crack and shatter. Similarly, the dour Josef is not used to laughing too much either, and his mirth sounds something akin to the rumble of a Bradley tank on its way to occupy a town.

The young student Tlaxlocaztla has not been so fortunate in her endeavors. She is having a hard time staying with Gordo, Regina, and their four young children.

"I can't sleep at night," she says. "We are all in the same room. Gordo snores loudly, the baby cries half the night, and there is something moving about above my head, a mouse or something.

At least I hope it's a mouse. Then Regina gets up at some unearthly hour to begin preparing tortillas, and wakes me up asking if I would like to help. I mean, I'm all down with helping around the kitchen, but grinding corn at 4 AM by candlelight is stretching it!"

I feel sympathy towards Tlaxlocaztla as she tries to rediscover her roots and re-establish a lost cultural heritage. As a Latina of Mexican descent growing up in the USA, she has suffered her fair share of alienation, but I fear she has come here with rose-tinted glasses regarding questions of identity and belonging. If she held expectations of being embraced with open arms by the local people as a prodigal daughter returning home, those illusions have come crashing down.

"They are incredibly kind and polite to me," she says, exasperated, "but I still feel...such a foreigner! Maybe it is because I don't speak Tzeltal."

And with that observation, I think she is beginning to understand the complexity of the indigenous identity in Chiapas. Like how the Mesoamerican Mayan civilization once spread across the whole region, crossing the national borders of Mexico, Guatemala,

Belize, and Honduras. Indeed Chiapas was part of Guatemala until it was annexed by Mexico in 1823, so to be indigenous in Chiapas is complicated. We ask the teacher Gordo his views on the issue.

"We are both indigenous Mayan and Mexican," he answers diplomatically. "We have equal solidarity and affinity to Mexico and to our indigenous brothers and sisters from other countries like Guatemala."

Meanwhile, Tlaxlocaztla, rootless, adrift, remains as much a caxlan, an outsider, in their eyes as much as, say, Josef from Poland.

•••

The end is in sight. The final coat of cement is applied to the tank. Nebula and Tlax suggest a plan to paint a mural with the children on the tank walls and the idea is a received warmly. Nebula, in spite of herself and her penchant for presenting herself as punk rock bitch from hell, has assumed a Mary Poppins-ish role with the children. They trail about her all day, and she keeps them laughing with her antics and humor. She has a sweet voice ("I used to sing with a hardcore band called Spyder Cunts. We rocked, man!") and teaches the children the ABC song like a Sesame Street character.

There's a good mood about today on the construction site and we make great progress. We are content in our work. Strangely, none of the women of the community have come out to see the tank. In other communities, the women and girls flock to see everything that is going on and to check out the visitors, to talk, inquisitive and bold. But here, it's like a community without women in public, or a community where the women stay in the shadows. Maria has been doing the rounds of the houses to check in with them, to talk to them about their water needs and what suggestions they have for the project, but not one has yet to come out to see the work. It is true it is not that interesting—just a bunch of men (and three caxlan women) mixing cement.

"Where are the women? Don't they want to see what's going on?" asks Sofia.

"They are busy working in the kitchen," comes the standard reply from Don Sisifo.

Tlaxlocaztla is frustrated.

"Do they ever leave the kitchen?" she asks, still pissed off that she has been unable to find a compañera who will submit to being interviewed for her field research. ("They claim that their Spanish isn't good enough, but I suspect the men are telling them not to do it," says the fiery student.)

"They work in the hortaliza too," says Don Sisifo, not quite getting the student's line of questioning.

It is an unhappy situation, but should we intervene or respect the usos y costumbres of the community?

"We should invite them to join us, right now," says Tlax.

Maria reins in the younger, hot-headed student. "We can ask for the issue to be brought up at the next community assembly."

Back on the coal front, many hands are making light work again. A gang of cheerful young tricksters work as they play and play as they work. These teenagers should rightly be in school, but there is no school, so they labor instead and they bring their youth to work. They discover fun in mixing cement and when they tire of that, there is always the caxlanes to make fun of.

I busy myself with cleaning up the mess the youngsters are making while mixing the cement. The compas don't tire of standing around commenting on my spade skills. "He can work!" they say in a tone of surprise, as if it was a miracle or something. The others paint the tank with cement water. The work on the walls inside the tank is almost complete. A couple more light coats with a brush, and then to begin on the floor.

Laying the final layer of the floor of the tank requires acrobatics. A youngster is hung from the hole of the tank by a rope and lowered into the ghastly chamber inside. There, suspended in mid-air, he has to drop a bucket of cement on the floor of the tank, and work it in with a trowel. The job is a process of elimination of ground space.

In an act that has his mates rolling around in laughter, the acrobat nearly throttles himself as the rope gets twisted. We let the youths work this out for themselves—educating themselves, as such. They tie together and hang some weird kind of trapeze in, and swing the young compañero on it, upside down through the little hole in the ceiling of the tank. Suspended in mid-air, he has to pat down the last bit of the floor in the tank. And at the end of his heroic and spectacular endeavour he is unceremoniously dragged out of the hole feet first. All very funny, and everybody cracks up. And it warms the cockles of my heart to see laughter bonding all the disparate people, beyond language or age.

So its 4 PM and we have finished, having applied the last touches on the tank; it's finally ready to fill with water. We connect the pipe to the entrance valve, embedded high up in the wall. It will take a whole night to fill up. These 13,000 liters of water will meet the village's daily needs. It's been a ton of work for thirty people. Almost two weeks of intense labor if you take into account the laying of the foundations. It now stands there, triumphant and proud, on top of a little hill in the center of the village, representing a grand step forward for this village of paltry material wealth.

And now it is noticeable that Don Sisifo is joining Alfredo in the league of sick water workers. Despite a fever, cough, and runny nose, he refuses to retire to his quarters to relax.

"But Don Sisifo," argues Maria, "you could pass it on to other people. Please, give yourself a break."

If daily life in the isolated Lacandon was not difficult enough, being sick really compounds the misery. Don Sisifo is absolutely miserable but, stubborn as a mule, he won't budge.

"No, we will just get this water system finished," he insists, coughing and spluttering, "and then I will rest."

We try to cheer him up, but only end up patronizing him. With the new water, we say, the incidence of sickness from water-related illnesses should plummet. The distribution tank, if treated with chlorine, can be a tool to combat outbreaks of water-bourn bacterial disease.

He smiles benevolently, as if he didn't know this.

"Yes, compañeros," he smiles, "yes."

"Although chlorine has a carcinogenic potential," chips in Josef.

"But carcinogenic risks are small in comparison to those related to inadequate disinfection," responds Maria.

Another argument develops. What began as an attempt to humor Don Sisifo ends up a ferocious argument between water team members, cumulating with an intervention from Don Sisifo.

"Compañeros, please, give yourselves a break. Less fights, let's all work together..."

The constant head-butting between Maria and Josef is becoming problematic. Indeed, the tension generated by Josef's belligerent attitude is casting a shadow over the dynamics and relationships within the whole group and, by default, negatively affecting the solidarity effort in general. How can we presume to help others if we can't even sort out our own basic internal relational problems? People don't have to necessarily like each other, but mechanisms must be put in place so that it doesn't impact the work.

The Josef problem comes to a head that very afternoon in an explosive outburst that ruptures the group irreversibly.

It begins with a silly practical joke. The compas came upon a small, highly poisonous snake wriggling around near the construction site. With a decisive strike of the machete, Vicente beheads the little viper. We all crowd around, fascinated. The body continues squirming for a little while after losing its head. It is a coral snake with a beautiful yellow, black, and red coat. Nebula picks up the remains of the snake and vows to make something creative with the skin.

Later, back in the schoolroom, everybody is chilling out after the day's work, lying around in hammocks, reading, writing, and chatting.

In retrospect, it is disputed as to exactly who came up with the devious prank, but Nebula says she thinks the idea was originally Tlaxlocaztla's, who denies this, counter-claiming that it was Nebula's, and that she merely went along with it. Nevertheless, they both accepted responsibility for the act.

Either way, the shiny, slimy carcass of the headless coral snake is placed in the creases of the makeshift pillow on Josef's bed.

"If he likes animals, he will love this," says Nebula, snickering somewhat cruelly.

Josef comes in shortly afterwards, fresh from his argument with Maria and still fuming. He ignores everyone, and gruffly retires to his bed to read. Everybody is in on the practical joke, and there is muffled laughter and titters and an air of expectation in the room. Omar has even set up his camera to record the whole gag. It should be pretty funny to see Josef's reaction to finding the dead snake on his pillow. Hilarious even.

Unperturbed, he lays his head on the pillow and flicks open his book. I always remember what he was reading: John Zerzan's *Elements of Refusal*.

And I always remember Tlaxlocaztla's muffled chortle as his free hand moved to scratch his head, tantalizingly close to the carcass. His fingers inch closer and suddenly come upon a warm, slimy object.

No one could have known that he had an unusually violent phobia of snakes, but that still doesn't excuse us all for playing such a rotten prank. He grabs the coral viper and slowly it registers in his brain what he is touching. His reaction is spectacular. He sits bolt upright, screams in horror, rolls off the makeshift bed with a crash, tossing the carcass away and continues screaming, his whole body shaking violently. We all burst into howls of laughter, a dam-bursting of pitiless hilarity.

"Smile you're on candid camera!" hoots Omar, moving in for a close up.

Josef snaps. He jumps up, snorting with rage, grabs Omar's camera and flings it against the blackboard, smashing it into a dozen pieces. Like an unbridled beast, he pushes Omar aside and stomps over to the uncontrollably giggling Nebula. With all his bodily force, he upends her bed, brutally tossing her on the dirt floor. Why her? Who knows?—we all were laughing.

Josef collapses onto the earthen floor himself, sobbing, and a quiet descends upon the shook-up schoolroom. Omar is picking up pieces of his smashed camera in utter disbelief, and a scraped and bruised Nebula is groaning a little as she picks herself up. Ironically, the headless snake lies tossed on the floor right beside the sniveling Josef and, upon noticing it, he cries out twice, a cry that is no more than a breath—"The horror, the horror."[2]

Josef moved out of the schoolroom that evening. He departed the delegation, but he didn't go too far—he went over to stay with our neighbors, Don Sisifo's family. Most of us are feeling remorseful and the mood is melancholic. It is Sofia who steps in and seeks resolution.

"That was really mean," she says. "We need to hold a group session to talk through this, and apologize to Josef."

"He had it coming, man," says Nebula, unrepentant. "He has been an asshole all this time, and he deserves it."

I'm a bit shocked by her callousness, but then again she is still hurting from being flung on the floor.

Anyway, he refuses to come join us for a group meeting.

"He says he is no longer part of this delegation," reports Sofia,

---

2. OK, I jest. He didn't repeat the infamous words of Kurtz in *Heart of Darkness*. He probably said something like Kurwa! which is how they say Fuck! in Polish. Nevertheless, it is a *Heart of Darkness* moment, that is all I'm trying to say.

the envoy. "He is staying on as a guest of the community and a compañero of Don Sisifo."

Fuck, what a mess. In the absence of the protagonist we carry on discussing the incident all night.

Tlax is equally unrepentant. "If was his own fault. If he wasn't so fucking uptight, the whole drama wouldn't have happened. I'm just sorry that Omar lost his camera."

Omar is philosophical. "Easy come, easy go, I probably needed a new one anyway."

Maria is more pissed about the effect this whole drama has had on the water project. It has been pretty much an exemplary job so far and now this has fucked things up. She is also stuck on the old arguments with Josef.

"He needs to learn some facts before he starts mouthing off all the time."

Me, I'm feeling indifferent. He would have my compassion but I just don't like the guy. My thoughts dwell on a different, if related theme. I'm haunted by Chinua Achebe's words in his critique of *Heart of Darkness*. "Can nobody see the preposterous and perverse arrogance in thus reducing Africa [read, the Lacandon] to the role of props for the break-up of one petty European?"

"It's always about us, isn't it?" I say. "Here we are all obsessing on our own little squabbles even when we come this far, about as far from our everyday lives as possible, here in the depths of the Lacandon Jungle and we can't escape our own psyches and egos. It's depressing, we are trying to change the world and we can't even begin to change ourselves."

Most everyone has some degree of objection to this assertion, and so the discussion goes on long into the night.

Heart of the Community

We all wake up late—the sun has already risen!—and rush through breakfast to get to work. The men are already up and running, and there is Josef, embedded in the compañeros' ranks and studiously ignoring the caxlanes.

The tank has completely filled with clear, lovely water and now we have to flush it out, and with the water, all the cement residue. Out floods the water through the exit valve and amusingly, everybody stares with quiet wonder, as if they had never seen a bit of water in their lives. But the thing is, after working so hard so long, it is a mesmerizing sight to behold! And we refill it again. That satisfying echo of cascading water filling the great cauldron.

And now time to put in my personal favorite part of the whole system—the ballcock, a device that will shut off the supply of the water when the tank is full. It's so simple and so fucking brilliant. Homage to the clever Persians who came up with this ingenious invention in the ninth century. It is basically a larger version of a float valve in a flush toilet. A valve is connected to the incoming water supply and is opened and closed by the lever which has the float mounted on the end. When the water level has risen to a preset fill line, the float forces the lever to close the valve and shut off the water flow. No overflows, no mess. Oh, if only there was such a ballcock mechanism for dealing with all life's little difficulties. We put the ballcock in, the water fills to the full level, and the tank is ...complete!

We are about to connect the first part of the distribution line, but before we proceed, the community wants to bless the water and tank. The *magrina* is called up from her kitchen. Lorena runs up the hill pulling off her apron and pulling on her posh shawl. Don Job assumes the role of *catequista*, and the two of them go about their celestial work with rigor. The short ceremony involves blessing the water, burning incense, and offering a few prayers. Everybody is very attentive and bows their heads. Not wishing to upset anyone, Praxedis and fellow atheist Sofia make themselves scarce during the ceremony, and begin to set up things for tomorrow's tap-stand workshop. The other water team crew busy themselves snapping photos, like a swarming paparazzi. Omar looks a little gloomy without his camera.

And so, religious duties concluded, off we go to begin the distribution line within the village, definitely the most exciting and fun part of the whole project. This involves running a line, or in this case two separate lines to the two distinct barrios of the community. The main lines of one-inch PVC traverse the main paths of the village, and then we put in a tee-valve outside every dwelling, and run a half-inch tube into the patio of each house. Maria and Praxedis had surveyed the layout of the community and have drawn up the most efficient layout design.

The first pipes of the village distribution system are laid out with mute fanfare. The men are digging trenches and we are unrolling the pipe and connecting them. There is a perceivable buzz, and the air is filled with an excited chatter. Children run around and the women are out of their kitchens and on their patios, preparing a spot for the tap-stand. Each house has paid their 100 pesos, which will get them the angular metal stand and tap, and the pipe and cement to make the base. The communal public stands don't get as much attention as the private ones.

How the children absorb and exude the mood! Like canaries in the mine, they send out advance signals, not of danger though, but of celebration. The community, this little village in the middle of nowhere, is emerging into a whole new era. No longer will the woman tramp down to the well or the river to get water; now they

will have the luxury and joy of stepping outside their kitchen and turning on the tap, and hey presto—water. A simple thing in life that everybody reading this book takes for granted. This is a great day for the community. Absolute happiness. Kids call out my name and I melt. There is a real sense that we've entered into the bosom of the community, into the hearts of the people.

Perched up on the hill, so gravity will do it's work, the tank looks quite majestic. We arrive in front of a house and begin connecting the tee and running a line into the patio. Everyone emerges from the kitchen to watch the work—the women with broad smiles on their faces, and older and infirm members of the family clearly content. And the children, their parents' excitement tangible, frolic about. When the water finally flows from the tap, everyone is delighted. Oh this glistening and gorgeous liquid—see it rushing out.

•••

Prefiguration is the political practice of employing the means to embody the end result.

So it is here. Laying the distribution line is painfully slow, because the *modus operandi* is not dictated by temporal constraints or costs of production, but rather it is about participation and process. In the water project, how we conduct the process is as important as the ends, because both are intrinsically linked. This prefigurative model is how practical autonomy functions. It may not be particularly efficient, but it is inclusive. We want everyone to know what is going on, what we are doing, and understand how it all works, each step of the way.

So, for instance, we work patiently in each house, locating the highest point of their patio for the tap-stand if they are located near the river, to avoid flooding, or the lowest point if their plot is on higher ground—so the water pressure will be greater. These are minute decisions that will affect the particular families for the rest of their lives, so we make decisions carefully.

The pressure is different in every tap, which means some families could have an abundant flow and other families further along the line would receive less. Praxedis and Maria set the flow on all the tap stands to one liter per eight seconds, which should address this problem, and yet still some families at the end of the line have very low flow. Unfortunately, there is nothing we can do about that. Ironically, the water responsable Vicente's plot is located at the end of the line and his flow is the worst in the whole community. He is crestfallen to see only a trickle flow out from his family plot's tap-stand. We recommend that he build a mini-tank to store water; fill it up at night, and use it during the day. We leave a little extra cement and rebar for him to do the work.

The tap in Don Sisifo's compound works fine but Josef discovers that the tee-connector is leaking about 50% of the water coming through. Josef is still in a huff and won't communicate with anybody except Sofia, who acts as mediator and tells Maria. Maria comes over and they evaluate the problem. It's the tee-connectors. They are cheap, poorly made, and leak. It is discouraging.

Maria resolves the situation temporarily by taping up the connection with copious amounts of water-resistant tape and promises to deliver better quality tees some time in the future. Everyone knows though, that now these tees are in place in the trench, soon to be dug in and covered, that nobody is going to dig them up again and change the connectors. So the tape is actually a long-term solution. The dilemma is that the water system won't be complete if we skip the tees for now, and everybody, both compañeros and water workers, really want to finish up this week! The thought of returning to San Cristobal to purchase better tees and coming back the following week is simply too exasperating.

"The tape should suffice," says Maria, with only a tiny hint of doubt in her voice. She advises the compas not to bury the connections, to leave it open to keep an eye on them.

Josef disagrees, and puts his case directly to Don Sisifo.

"We should not connect the distribution line until we have good connectors. We should wait."

But in this case, Don Sisifo's word is final. He too is excited by the prospect of the whole project being complete within a couple of days.

"No. Let's work with what we have. Tape it up. It is what the people want. They are happy to have water arriving into their houses."

Praxedis holds the tap-stand workshop outside the bodega, assisted by Sofia—they are inseparable. It is not rocket science, just a lesson in how to connect all the various plumbing bits and pieces to put together the tap-stand, and then a demonstration of how to make a simple cement mount, using a wooden mould, to protect the tubing. I drop over to see how they are getting on and there is that quiet hum of industrious men playing around with tools and metal things—all good. They really get into it and seem keen to learn, like people hungry for more and more knowledge. I am also particularly glad to see that Alfredo, the water responsable, has made an appearance today, his first venture outdoors since he was struck down with illness last week.

"How are you, compañero?"

"*Mas o menos*," he says, putting a brave smile on it. He does look pale and drawn still, but he has come out to join in the excitement of the moment. Or maybe he felt guilty because the other compañeros were covering for him, digging the trench leading into his family compound? Nevertheless, it's good to see him back on his feet again.

Adelita's brother also attends the workshop. I ask him how his mother, Doña Consuela, is getting on. She is back from hospital and in bed at home, being tended to by Adelita, he reports. We vow to visit her that evening.

Meanwhile Tlaxlocaztla, Nebula, and Omar have mustered up a group of kids and have begun to prepare the tank surface for painting the mural. The kids are busy preparing potential designs on scraps of paper. Marisol is leading the way with sketches of flowers and butterflies; Jorge with armed, masked Zapatista soldiers; Luis with helicopters; and Frida, a seven-year-old with some artistic flair, has drawn up some pretty impressive rivers flowing through mountains. A lovely wide-eyed boy, called Cuitláhuac, paints the moon and the stars. All the designs will be incorporated one way or another, so that it is truly a collaborative effort.

I've been assigned by Maria to go check on the spring box. I ask for somebody to accompany me on the task, and am I'm secretly delighted that Nebula jumps at the opportunity. She may come across as a little bit off her rocker, but I like her mischievous Mary Poppins spirit and dark sense of humor.

So we set off on the trail up the mountain, light and flirtatious. I remember treading this same path for the very first time two and a half months previous. It was a dark and intimidating uncut terrain, and we pioneers fought our way through undergrowth with machete in hand. Now there is a covered trench nestling the water pipes, and the passage feels familiar. True enough, I have walked it about 1,001 times, and dug in at a variety of points along the trench, and I am intimate with each curve and hill and ditch and ravine. It is a strange phenomenon to be so familiar with a piece of earth so far from my own home, land, place. But it feels as welcoming as any patch of land in Ireland, and makes me feel content to be grounding myself with the one, holy, and eternal living entity— Gaia—*madre tierra, pachamama.*

"Don't be such a fucking hippy," protests Nebula, unimpressed by my pantheistic musings. "Hey, hand over the chili sauce, time to lube this boy up."

We have arrived at the exposed section of pipe by the river where we had the mole problem. There are no signs of newly-chewed pipe—it seems that Praxedis's salsa mix is keeping the moles at bay for now. We apply the chili sauce liberally, and move on up the trail.

Walking, we ask questions. Like how did Nebula first get involved in the Zapatistas?

"My sex-workers' collective were sending money to Chiapas."

Of course. Explain?

Nebula goes on to quickly outline a brief personal history of an unconventional upbringing: moving from place to place, leaving school early, the punk life, drugs, traveling a lot, squatting in Barcelona, manic-depressive disorder, joining a circus ("my specialty was juggling with fire upside-down on a trapeze while singing Gloria Gaynor's 'I Will Survive'"). Later she made her living by subjecting herself to human research experiments.

"But fuck that, man. Being a guinea pig is no fun, so I started dancing. Hooked up with the local anarcha sex-workers' co-op and found out about Chiapas. There was a real buzz about what the Zapatistas were doing and loads of people were making the obligatory pilgrimage. I saved up some cash and here I am."

Is it all you expected?

"It's a mind fuck, so confusing, but yeah, I'm down with the program. I don't know about the peace camps, they suck, but working on the water project is awesome."

Before coming to work on the water project, Nabula had stayed in a peace camp for a month. The role of internationals is to monitor the military presence, and since this particular community was high in the mountains, traffic through the place was rare.

Maybe one army truck passed through every few days. The rest of the time, the volunteers were confined to the environs of the peace camp and interaction with the general community was minimal.

"I got to read a lot of books, but I was bored shitless," explains Nebula. The problem with the peace camps is the separation from the daily life of the village; working on a water project means being right in the center of community life.

The spring bower is as cool and seductive as ever. Moist with verdant growth and fragrant air. The spring wall has not held up too well, and rocks have fallen out with the increasing pressure of the water. We patch it up, using even heavier stones, and packing them in more closely. Otherwise the pool is relatively clean, but it still needs a laminated roof to keep the falling leaves and debris out. Must remember to tell Maria to add that to the growing list of outstanding things to buy.

We check the plumbing. The outlet pipe seems fine, and the exit valve seems to be functioning well. "Let me just check if I can turn it off and on, OK?" and as I turn the lever slowly, the fucking thing snaps off in my hand!

"Oh fuck!"

"Damn it man, what the fuck are you doing?" scolds Nabula. "Haven't you ever heard of the saying that if it's not broken, don't fix it!!"

"Well too late now."

Man, this sucks, me and my fucking tinkering. Have I fucked up the whole water system?

Fortunately, upon closer inspection, we discover the open/close mechanism is still working, one just needs to use a wrench to adjust it. That is alright then. Or even better, because it means kids can't mess around with it and turn the water supply off by mistake.

All's well that ends well!

"Dude, you are so fucking lucky," says Nebula. "There are some very serious consequences for sabotaging the peoples' water system, you know. You could have been tied to a tree all night in the jungle!"

"Yeah, yeah I know. But you were an accomplice. You would be there with me."

"A night in the jungle with you? I could handle that," she says with a smile.

And that remark, so laden with promise, fills me with gladness.

· It's a fine thing to see that face-shattering, rapturous smile on Don Sisifo's visage as we return to the community, signifying in some sense—despite everything, the faulty tees or whatever else—that all is well. The whole system is in place, the distribution line is nearly finished. In the patios of the houses, people are gathered around the temporary tap-stands, filling buckets, washing babies, filling their cupped hands with sparkling water, just fetishizing the precious liquid. Sun shines, water flows, laughter abounds.

It is for this day that we climbed mountains knee deep in mud; endured unrelenting mosquitoes and chaquista attacks; roared with pain as our hands tore in pieces to push the pipe connections together; plagued ourselves with technical problems that threatened the whole project; breathed in the noxious fumes of the cement in cloistered pandemonium; were incarcerated in a tomb-like tank in the high heat of day; braved snakes, scorpions, crocodiles, tarantulas, wild cats; sweated, bled, shat water; spent feverish long nights; engaged the twitchy young soldiers at checkpoints; faced deportation; fought bitter internal strifes amongst ourselves; fell so low; washed in mud; ate shit; tolerated endless teasing; put up with foolishness; traveled along tortuously hacked up pathways all night long; crossed potential paramilitary enclaves... All for this. The system is complete. There are a few glips, but it is functioning fine; each house is receiving their water. The people are happy. The children are laughing. As I walk between the school and the kitchen I can't stop myself crying a little, tears of simple joy. It is an emotional time. How much romance can one man take?

And us, the water team, are out of here soon. Such is international solidarity—we are the ones who leave. The tanks and tubes and piped water will remain, and the people will remain, and we will move on to the next project, the next set of challenges. The pirate life, up and down the canyons, plumber by day, clandestine by night.

A party is being organized for tomorrow—our last day. The announcement brings happiness for most, but terror for a few. The pigs that roam the community in a procession of indiscriminate foraging seem to sense the impending doom for one amongst their number. We volunteers have gotten to know the community pigs quite well, as they rummage around the schoolroom, by the river, and loiter around our kitchen. We have bestowed such love/hate names on each as Bush (the dumb one), Cheney (the mean one), Condi (the sneaky one), and Rumsfeld (the vicious one). Today a pig is getting neutered nearby and he cries like a little baby, and even squeals like a pig. Who is it? Bush? Cheney? Nope, the vicious pig Rumsfeld is getting his nuts cut off and nobody is losing sleep over that.

Tonight we are holding the final assembly, where we'll wrap things up, plan for the future, go over a few details for tomorrow's fiesta, and listen to the compañeros. As everybody files into the schoolroom I am glad to see Josef enter, looking less grim-faced than usual. Now that he is back in the schoolroom—the scene of the crime, such as it is—maybe we can have some reconciliation.

Josef aside, the dominant vibe is demure satisfaction. Maria calls everyone to order and starts the meeting. Then she pauses and invites Don Sisifo to start instead.

"Thank you compañera. But, please, go ahead..."

Maria begins again, launching into a talk about the basic tools and materials we are going to leave behind for any future repairs of the system. Mid-sentence, suddenly she stops. Everybody follows the direction of her stare. A group of compañeras, led by Adelita, are walking through the doorway.

"Welcome, compañeras!" says Maria, the thrill in her voice reflecting the general delight among us volunteers to see the women.

The women are here to argue the case for putting a tap stand for washing clothes in the center of the community. They had prioritized this, but the plans went ahead without taking their desires into consideration.

Don Sisifo disagrees with this suggestion: "The women can wash clothes in the river like always."

A debate strikes up in Tzeltal.

The student Tlaxlocaztla interrupts, asking for a translation so that everybody can participate. Gordo obliges.

A compañera named Lorena raises her voice and speaks for a few minutes in Tzeltal.

"The compañera says that the women find it hard to wash clothes down in the river during the rainy season. It's too muddy," says Gordo.

"And?" asks Tlaxlocaztla. "Gordo, the compañera said a lot and you only translated one sentence!"

Gordo looks like a recalcitrant schoolboy and promises to try to translate in full.

So what should have being a straightforward community assembly to wrap things up and express gratitude, instead evolves into a vital encounter between the women and the men. Later, reflecting upon our time here, everybody in the water team expresses satisfaction that we played some small role in facilitating this development. As it is, the debate about locating a communal tap in the center is resolved with accommodation of the women's proposal. Furthermore, due to the women raising their voices, they were able to push through their demand for a woman to represent their interests on the water committee—thereby breaking the glass ceiling to what previously was considered a male preserve. It's an exciting assembly.

Tlaxlocaztla can't contain her delight: "Right on, sisters!" she shouts out.

Deep in the night, Don Sisifo sums up the meeting and brings it to a conclusion.

"The community is very happy with the water. We are very content and honored that you came to our community and gave us this solidarity. Thank you for your gift to the community. Thank you for coming to this poor corner of Chiapas and helping us. You are always welcome back here."

Everybody gives us a round of applause.

His words are fond and generous, especially considering he is such a quiet man. We are all chuffed, but, his words bother me a little. Does he get it? Does he get that we are not here as an act of charity or to provide a service in the absence of government works or schemes? That we are here not just to help poor people, but we do it as a contribution to the broader revolutionary project of autonomy? That our solidarity is not just giving them something quintessential that they lack, but a contribution to something beyond ourselves, beyond this village, and indeed beyond the whole Lacandon region?

Or, conversely, is he the insightful one? Are we deceiving ourselves? Are we autonomous global rebels, or are we more like a group of militant Mother Theresas?

We have delivered on the water project, but did we go wrong somewhere in our efforts to build a real solidarity between different people sharing similar political goals?

Praxedis steps up to thank the community for receiving us, and to reiterate the same words he said when we arrived. This time he asks Gordo to translate, hoping his point will be understood.

"We were not sent here to 'give' you solidarity, compañeros and compañeras. We are not a service provider. We are not policing international aid funds, nor are we fulfilling our mandate for an aid agency. This is not charity, we came here in the spirit of solidarity to share, to reach towards a sense of reciprocity. For us, international solidarity is being in the same struggle, together."

Despite the eloquent words, repeated again, I'm not sure they are achieving their desired aim. Nobody responds. It is as if the compas eye him suspiciously. As if they were saying to themselves: "We are not the same! We are not equal! You are caxlanes, the world is yours. We are indigenous, we know nothing but dispossession and abandonment. We are not together in the same struggle, we are different. Our struggle is ours, and yours is yours."

These are my speculations. Of course I don't know what the compañeros are thinking. There is just this silence, this edge in the air.

The community assembly quickly turns to other business.

By this time, I have had enough of the meeting and the claustrophobic schoolroom. I abdicate all responsibility and escape outside to the rising moon, resplendent over the enchanting valley, and kick ball with the gaggle of little boys and girls who are lingering still, despite the late hour.

Such a resplendent night is an appropriate setting for a fine act of generosity. Omar approaches Josef as he leaves the schoolroom on his way back to Don Sisifo's. I am hoping that he is not going to slap him around the place for smashing up his camera.

"Josef, I want to apologize for the silly prank and the way we treated you."

Josef looks uncertain. Is this another trick? Is he about to fall for another mean prank?

Omar looks at him with clear and honest eyes. "I speak from here," he says, touching his chest, "and I hope you will forgive me for my part in the practical joke."

Josef acknowledges the apology with a grunt.

"It's alright."

And as he turns to go, he looks back.

"Sorry for destroying your camera."

"That's cool man, cool," says Omar, and peacefully wanders back into the schoolroom. Sometimes dignity springs from the humblest of acts.

Inspired by Omar, I too step up to offer my apologies. "Josef!..." I call out, but he is already receding into the great darkness. Ah fuck it, I'll do it tomorrow. Or sometime.

Springtime in Zapatistalandia

So the big day has finally arrived—the inauguration party for the community water system. The mood is serene and the workload light. Almost everything is ready and we have just a little fine tuning to oversee on the pipe network.

After breakfast, a few of us linger around the table, chatting and sipping coffee.

"So are we gonna have the best party of our lives tonight?!" asks Nebula, excited at the prospect of her first fiesta in insurgent lands.

"Zapatistas throw great insurrections," says Praxedis, "but terrible parties."

"Sad but true," I concur.

Nebula says we are "miserable fuckers."

"No, really," I argue. "Every time we complete a water system, the community celebrates by holding a fiesta. I am as fun loving and decadent as the next party animal, but these events are an ordeal, the equivalent of an evening in a dentist's waiting room or even a glimpse of purgatory. But I have met several caxlanes who have attended many more community fiestas than I, and even enjoyed some of them, so who am I to critique? Everyone's different."

Maria chimes in. "The people in the community love them though, Ramon, and everybody gets all excited at the prospect of the night's revelry. And true enough, it does drag on to the dawn, and people do dance all night, but it's definitely a different pace and atmosphere to what a caxlan might expect. Maybe because there is no booze."

"No, it is not just the lack of alcohol that leads to dull parties," I argue. "Fiestas in non-Zapatista indigenous communities can be wild and unhappy affairs, depending on the amount of Pox that has been drunk."

"Pox?!" interrupts Nabula. "People drink pox? I am missing out on something here."

"No no, pox is an appropriately named evil liquor," I explain. "Distilled locally from sugarcane. Sometimes pronounced 'posh.' It is highly intoxicating and induces an appalling drunken stupor."

"Damn, I need to get my hands on some of this stuff," says Nebula. "Sounds awesome..."

"Pox abuse of course gives rise to a lot of social problems," adds Maria. "The Zapatista ban in their base communities has been instrumental in building community cohesion and reducing incidents of familial or social violence."

"Even so," I continue, "beyond the welcome absence of pox, fiestas in the communities can be torridly dull affairs. I will be sneaking off to read my book as soon as the wretched event begins."

Gordo, the maestro, walks in at this moment, to drop off a pile of freshly cooked tortillas.

He is ebullient, and smiles widely.

"Are you looking forward to the fiesta tonight, compa?" he asks me eagerly.

"Oh yeah, I can't wait," I respond, somewhat sheepishly.

"Ramon was just saying that he is a party animal and he is going to rock out tonight—until the dawn!" says Nebula, mischievously.

Gordo claps me on the back, enthusiastically.

"That's fantastic, Ramon!"

"I will tell the community that you are going to dance all night. The people will be very happy to see that."

He shimmies out the door, swinging his hips, doing a pretend dance.

"*Ramon el mero bailarín!*" He hoots with laughter. Ramon the great dancer!

"Fucking Nebula," I hiss, as the others fall about the place laughing.

But despite my reservations, this particular fiesta comes as a pleasant surprise to me. Like a world turned upside down—something I could never have imagined—we have a marvelous party... Although not at the main event, but a clandestine offshoot.

The day passes in an industrious spirit. We're getting lots of little bits and pieces done, fine tuning this and that. Helping people construct their family tap stands, digging here and there, testing the pressure, tightening valves. A group of women come together during the morning to put together a tap stand for the collective clothes washing area. We earmark a bag of cement—the very last one—for the later construction of a large concrete washbasin. The day is punctuated by minor moments of crisis—people coming up and saying that the water isn't arriving to their house—but it is usually just a blocked pipe or a faulty connection. Really, the system is almost flawless and works perfectly fine; it's been an exemplary project. The community are delighted with us and we are greeted by smiles and handshakes everywhere we go. Like Springtime in Zapatistalandia.

The volunteers cook a last communal lunch together. We are a happy group of disparate international people, brought together, if not entirely randomly, at least arbitrarily, and we've found common ground and built a temporary autonomous zone of tight comradeship. So even if our attempts at building solidarity with the Zapatistas has been potted, at least we can take comfort in the solid bonds we've built among our small group.

"How can I ever return to the office after an experience like this?" laments Sofia. "I will go stircrazy."

Omar didn't get his documentary film recorded, but he is philosophical: "I am beginning to learn to see with my eye and not just through the lens. It is a rich experience."

Tlaxlocaztla didn't get all the interviews she needed, but she is confident she can cobble a good paper together with her copious notes and observations. For her, it has being a tumultuous learning experience, getting to know "her" people and feeling pride for Mexican and indigenous culture.

"Despite all the challenges I didn't expect, or maybe because of them, it's like I am discovering a whole new me, an awakening of my true hybrid identity."

Our last lunch together is interrupted by an unmerciful racket outside the kitchen. The two Galician fishermen are dragging a pig, the chosen one, away for slaughter. The pig is thrashing about with all its considerable strength and squealing like, well, a stuck pig.

Who is it?

"They are off to butcher Baby Bush," Praxedis informs us.

"Oh, I thought they would kill Cheney, the fat one. He seems about ready."

"Oh no, fat Cheney is their prize pig," chimes in Maria. "Worth a lot of money in the market. Baby Bush is like the runt of the pack, the one who didn't develop as well as the rest. Maybe a bit retarded."

"For a vegetarian, you seem to know a lot about offing pigs," notes Omar.

"The Revolution has come," hums Nebula, remembering the old Black Panther ditty, "Off the pigs!"

"Good song, you must teach the kids that one," says Omar.

A few of us follow the Galician fishermen up to their house to witness the slaughter, joining a gaggle of kids and a pack of dogs. We are enthralled as the living beast is stripped to a bare-boned carcass in less than half an hour. First they tip the struggling pig onto its back, four men each hold a leg, and a fifth plunges a knife through his heart. Blood spurts out and the dogs go loopy with bloodlust, and Bush shudders into death, choking and snorting. Finally he is still. Quickly, the compañeros set upon the carcass with flaming sticks of ocote, burning off all the hair. Now the pig is naked white, sad to behold, and wretched. One of the Galician fishermen wields a long, ornate knife and, with much dexterity, skins the beast, peeling off the oily flesh to reveal the fatty meat below. The thick blubbery white substance is cut off and tossed to the drooling dogs, and they snarl and fight over the scrapings, frantically devouring their portion.

Gordo provides some commentary as the butchering continues. "The pig is worth about 9 pesos a kilo in the market in Ocosingo; this one weighs about 55 kilos, I would say."

So this pig would have gotten the community about 450 pesos ($45 US). Baby Bush was about eight months old—eight months foraging, snorting, shitting, and being chased by the community's army of scruffy dogs. The short and violent life of a free-range Lacandon pig. That said, these pigs have it a lot better than their fellow creatures in the industrial pig factories, free, as they are, to roam around the community day and night, jumping into the river, foraging around the forest—the unfettered ecstasies of a free range hog.

"The pigs are one of the people's few sources of cash income," explains Gordo. "The big fat ones may be 100 kilos [2 cement bags] which is almost 1,000 pesos [$100 US]."

And how many pigs does the community have?

"This community has seven. They represent almost the total income for the year. We have plenty of chickens too. They are worth about 35 pesos each in the market—not much."

"Even as free-range chickens?" asks Sofia.

But there is no free-range market. All chickens are sold by weight, not rearing conditions. And with the money earned from selling the livestock, the community buys tools, utensils, clothes, rubber boots, and whatever else is needed. It's a small pot of income for a wide range of necessities.

I ruminate on the scant economy of a peasant. Even if they manage to sell a bit of corn or labor a little, the income is negligible. It is hard to figure out how they survive year in, year out.

There is good news regarding the fiesta later this evening: the hired musician has not turned up. OK, this is bad news for most, but I'm of the opinion that 75% of the problem with campo fiestas stems from the exploits of the godforsaken hired musician. Somewhere along the line, the entertainment industry in the outback of the Lacandon Rainforest got bogged down into the form of a tone-deaf machine operator with an electronic synthesizer. This infamous figure—"the musician"—drags his electric equipment along the length and breadth of these pristine jungle-based communities, turning his thirty-year-old synthesizer to top volume and proceeding to assault the people's listening sensibilities with a playlist of turgid tunes emanating from the tilted imagination of a discordant, crazed music-hater.

But the show must go on. By late afternoon everything is all set and the ceremony begins.

The whole community gathers in the church and sets off on a winding parade that goes up to the spring and weaves its way back to the distribution tank. The people, all wearing their Sunday best, are led by the *catequista* and *magrina* decked out in ceremonial robes, and flanked by flag bearers, holding Mexican tricolors high in the air. Older members of the community thump away on small hand-held drums and one plays a rustic, twangy guitar. One woman holds a large portrait of the Virgin of Guadalupe, and another, a metal cross. The colorful parade arrives at the tank, and a couple of firecrackers are set off. Incense fills the air with a pungent, otherworldly aroma. The ritualistic blessing of the water and the tank is overseen again by the magrina, Doña Lorena, and the elderly catequista, Don Corleone, and holy water is sprinkled all over the tank and those assembled. The congregation divides, by gender, into two groups, reciting prayers in unison. Six older men and women—the village elders—garbed in white ceremonial dress appear. To the tune of the twangy guitar, a scratchy fiddle, and a well-worn drum, they begin a strange and lilting dance, shuffling from one foot to the other while chanting esoteric words, eyes shut as if in an ecstatic reverie. It is a quietly mesmerizing ceremony, the purpose of which is to bless the water supply and ensure that the god of water—or some such immanent deity—is satisfied by the pious devotion of the villagers.

All this is much more than avowed atheists and simple philistines like Praxedis, Sofia, and I can handle, so we retreat to the far

bushes to sit down, have a smoke and chat. Tlaxlocaztla, Nebula, and Omar love it though. They lap up every moment, entranced as if they were witnessing some kind of clandestine Hermetic Order of the Golden Dawn liturgy. Maria, I notice, is in heated conversation to the side with Josef, sorting things out, I presume. Business over mysticism for them.

More fireworks are let off—to stir up the gods, Gordo tells us—and the elaborate and archetypal ritual is concluded. The crisp national tricolor's are lowered and rolled up until the next occasion.

Visitors and guests from other communities are arriving—relatives, friends, compañeros, and some youth who are just along for the party—swelling the numbers in the village to a hundred or more. It is unsettling to mingle with unfamiliar compañeros in this, by-now, familiar place, but it is also interesting to watch the socializing. As usual, people are very reserved, modest, and quiet in their interactions, but the hum of Tzeltal fills the air and the mood is peaceful, engaging.

It's time to eat. The pork boils merrily in a huge cauldron that's balanced precariously upon a hefty log fire. It looks pretty diabolical, all the greasy fat and blubber gurgling in the blackened cauldron, but it smells quite fetching. Women serve lavish mugfuls of sugared corn porridge that is surprisingly delicious, and tamales and tortillas with beans are also on the menu. But it is the slaughtered pig that is the main culinary attraction and everybody lines up in anticipation of a plate full of boiling-hot swine broth. For a people whose consumption of meat is infrequent, this is a big event. We caxlanes feel guilty digging into the people's pork dish, since we really don't want it. Half of us are vegetarians or non-pork eaters, and the other half no fans of such rugged delicacies. Mostly though, we simply don't want to deprive any of these pork lovers their fill. But to decline this great gesture of the pig sacrificed in our honor would be insulting to the community. We have to appear to enjoy and, indeed, cherish the dish. In a carefully choreographed move, the vegetarians and non-pork eaters shuffle their plates around, and remove larger pieces of pork and hand them, surreptitiously, to me. I brought along a clean plastic bag, into which I pop the pieces of pork in order to dole out to folks later, maybe in the form of tacos prepared in our kitchen. Nevertheless, vegetarian or not, everyone has to try the food and be seen to sip the broth and comment on its delectable richness: protocol, and respect for the effort the people went to at least demands that. Maria shares her plate with the faithful Marisol, who is seated by her side, and Omar makes a big deal of passing out chunks of pork to the compañeros around him, telling them that, in his religion, pork is special and, in order to purify the soul, must not be eaten.

As darkness falls, the women collect the licked-clean plates. It is now time for the party proper to begin. Mercifully, there is still no sign of the demonic electronic synthesizer or its dreaded operator. We will be treated to some community theater, poetry, acoustic music, and dance.

Everyone sits on rough benches, or planks placed on boxes, around the basketball court. All the villagers are here—young, old, women and men. Gentle, understated, quiet and demure. Under a great star-strewn sky, the community comes together to celebrate its survival and consolidation, and the new water system. It is a powerful moment.

The show begins as the same elderly dancers in their traditional costume face each other in a line and step around, nimble-footed, in unison—a move one water worker has amusingly described as the bus-stop shuffle. Indeed, the restricted movement of the dance makes a traditional stilted Irish catholic *ceili* seem like wild break-dancing by comparison. The guitar twangs, and drums keep the beat, and a man sings a melancholic lament while the children run around laughing in the background. Everybody claps graciously. Next up, a gaggle of young girls sing together in Tzeltal, half of them ready to drop dead on the spot from embarrassment. Once the tune is done though, they fall around the place giggling, but proud to have done it. Everyone claps in appreciation. To the delight of the children, a *piñata* is brought out and the kids spend a riotous ten minutes beating it to smithereens with a stick, and thumping the candy out. We, the water team, had packed the piñata with all the supplies, knowing that it was a surefire party favorite. General mayhem engulfs the basketball court as the piñata finally bursts and all the candy explodes onto the ground. We have to intercede, to dig out smaller children from the ferocious scrum of kids scrambling for the last *chicle*. A Robin Hood kind of operation is then conducted by the adults to ensure all children get a fair share of the spoils.

Oh no! He has finally arrived: the organ-grinder. He is snazzily dressed in an oversized silver zoot suit and sports prominent side-burns, immediately earning himself the moniker "Elvis" from our group. There is a ripple of excited banter as the musician sets up his equipment. The youth start acting giddy, and throngs of teenage girls bunch together in preparation for the onslaught. The gasoline-operated power source kicks in, the noise of its motor drowning out everything until the dreaded sound of over-amplified keyboard springs into life with an inferno of noise pollution. The organ-grinder launches into a song and, considering the cacophonous racket, it would seem that Elvis is playing the synthesizer with his forehead.

Soon enough, the dancing begins and the teenagers take over and play out the trials and errors of young romance in full view of parents, grandparents, and indeed, the whole community, who are seated quietly around the shadows of the basketball court. Mobs of young men and boys swarm over any perceived-available female at the start of each song and she must chose one of all her ardent admirers for the ensuing number. While the cacophony blasts unceasingly, the dance floor fills with standoffish young people swaying from side to side, not quite dancing but definitely not stationary. One could drive a bus in the space between the boy and girl dancers. It has begun, and it won't stop until the cocks start crowing. The dogs and sundry livestock have already departed the center of the community in protest of the electronic rumpus.

We, the caxlanes mess around the edge of the basketball court, mostly rocking out with the children. Kid-magnet Nebula has them all line-dancing and doing a kind of swing that has absolutely nothing to do with the dirge coming from the speakers. Occasionally we will indulge in a decorous dance in the shadows, so as not to disturb the universe. Maybe the older folks would disapprove if they saw us holding each other as we play-danced.

Such deliberations are brushed aside as the children surround us and drag us out to dance in the center of the basketball court. Under a sole naked bulb dangling forlornly from a rope, we groove around the place. Nebula is especially spectacular in her dancing skills as she swings a good half-dozen ragamuffin kids around the dance floor, mesmerizing young and old alike. I am somewhat maliciously trying to convince Praxedis to ask young Dolores for a dance but I'm sure one or both of them would die of mortification if such an appalling vista were to occur. Lola, anyway, is more than busy with a handful of suitors clambering for her presence on the dance floor. Both Praxedis and Sofia are too shy to ask one another to dance, so Omar does the decent thing and induces both to dance with him, and then deserts them on the dance floor together. But that doesn't succeed either; they both flee.

The din blares on, and the night sky is vast. The youngsters will dance late into the night. In this small community, deep in the rainforest, traditions remain strong. Despite the strong sugary sodas we are consuming, everyone is feeling bored and ready to leave. I am talking to Alfredo, now somewhat recovered from his illness, and it is a pleasant conversation until he asks me for some money to bring his sick child to the clinic in Ocosingo. Maybe he heard that Maria gave Doña Consuela money for her journey to the clinic. This is why we have the protocol that caxlanes don't give money to individual community members: it just causes more complications and awkward moments like this one.

"I can't, Alfredo. It's against the rules. I'm sorry."

And at that moment, I spot Adelita passing by with a tired, crying child in tow.

"Adelita! How is your mother getting on?"

Adelita looks distressed. "She is not getting better. The health responsable says we need to bring her back to hospital in Ocosingo."

"I'm sorry, Adelita, that's very tough for Doña Consuela and for you. If we can do anything to help...?"

Yes, she says, but doesn't say that they need money for transport. Alfredo's standing here too. I suggest that we should talk before we all leave in the morning, and excuse myself. It's too grim.

I return to the caxlan gang. They look bored and sugared-out from all the soda and cookies they've devoured in the absence of party drinks or cocktails.

"Let's sneak off to the river," suggests Nebula, and everybody delights at the idea... Except Maria, who feels inclined to stay— someone has to represent, she says. There's Josef, of course, who's embedded himself with a bunch of Don Sisifo's extended family and has been vigilantly avoiding the caxlanes all night anyway.

The six of us depart quietly into the darker shadows of the night, and make our way by flashlight to the riverbank. It is such a relief to be away from the maddening noise of the synthesizer, and be by the calm river on this warm tropical night. The water is glistening and gorgeous, it moves gracefully in one great unified body, in the moonlight, made up of an infinity of dancing light. In the air, there is a mood of mischievousness, born of our celebration of the project's completion and the group dynamic, which is intimate and fond. By the river, the mosquitoes and chaquistas are scarce, and the water is inviting, beguiling. We all so want to jump in.

Nebula looks at Tlaxlocaztla with a glint in her eye.

"You in?"

"Yeah, let's do it!"

The two of them lead the way, boldly stripping naked and wading into the river.

"It's fucking gorgeous!"

"It's awesome! Come on in."

I can't remember who was the next to undress and enter the inviting water, but everybody else follows suit quickly enough. We splash and cavort around in the breathtakingly fresh, mild water, which seems perfect on a balmy night like this.

It doesn't matter to us right now that we are breaking rules, taboos, and re-enforcing all the differences between us and the community—so be it. We are different, and difference is alright. This little act of boldness—nude civil disobedience in a sense—is not a two-fingers to the community and their usos y costumbres, but a little social rebellion against a superannuated and prudish custom that we don't agree with. Nobody can see us and nobody gets offended as we cavort in the river, splashing about and playing games. And anyway, I reckon very few people in the community would deny us our inoffensive, indulgent pleasure.

As the clothes go, we shed, too, our inhibitions. It is great to see Praxedis and Sofia finally consolidating timid desires—kissing and embracing in waist-high water. The rising moon reflects upon their glistening, beautiful forms. The semi-translucent night light coats them in soft azure tones, creating a picture of serene brilliance. The flow of water laps against their bodies.

"Ugh, gross," comments Nebula, noticing the romantic couple making out. "Get a room."

We emerge, water dripping from our bodies and, somewhat decadently, laze around the sandy bank *au natural*, enjoying the sultry night. I don't know if I ended up beside Nebula or she ended up beside me, but it is lovely to hold her in my arms, her wet skin tantalizing to touch—although I do have to take care not to get caught in any of her multiple metal piercings.

"Ugh, double gross," laughs Tlaxlocaztla, winking at Nebula.

From digging ditches and mixing cement to feral romance and torrid kissing under the stars, this water project is exceeding all expectations.

We can still hear the faint din of the synthesizer even here down by the river; it is but a distant reverberation. And suddenly it goes quiet.

"Compañeros and compañeras, listen up!"

We hear the voice of Don Sisifo loud and clear through the amplified speaker system.

"We are here now to give thanks to the compañeros of the water team. If they could all step up here now and receive the gratitude of the community."

A round of applause breaks out.

Oh fuck!

We are all lying around naked on a riverside beach like debauched libertines and the community is giving us a gracious round of applause from afar.

Nobody moves. We look at each other bemused. Instantaneously, everybody just explodes into riotous laughter. I have never cried with laughter with a bunch of naked water volunteers, but this project is a first in many ways.

This is also the moment that Maria comes running down to find us. She bursts through the blanket of trees hollering, "Compas! Hurry up, our presence is required..."

She stops at the sight of us.

"What the fuck?!"

And then she breaks up into bellowing laughter too.

Somewhat shame-facedly, we face the community—fully clothed now, of course. All the demure thanks are said, everyone full of humble words, thanking each other for this and that. It's all in good spirit and politeness. I wonder what they really think of us. We are, after all, just the most recent representatives of the class and race of people who have fucked them over since time began. But cautious people like these don't bite the hand that feeds. They certainly wouldn't tell us what they really felt about us.

Our only indication comes later when Gordo speaks to us with a wistful sigh:

"So you are leaving in the morning. Will you take me to San Cristobal with you? Take me to the United States or Italy?" He laughs ironically. "It is well for you people who can leave."

"Yes, we are the people that leave."

And we all know that tomorrow night we are all going to party like bikers in San Cristobal. We are going to get loaded, drink and dance all night, unleashing our more degenerate and unfettered sides. After this few weeks sojourn in pastoral tranquility, everyone is ready to let loose. And it is inconceivable that we would party with these compas in the same manner. Taking a bong hit with Don Sisifo, or doing a line with Adelita stretches the imagination. These are lines in the sand that further emphasize the differences between us, that make building that genuine horizontal and unmediated reciprocal relationship even more difficult.

Reciprocity, for people from different places and cultures to come together as one in common struggle is a fine idea and a grand aspiration. While the solidarity is there between us, as we share concrete goals, I fear reciprocity is, in instances like this, a bridge too far. We are bringing different capacities to the banquet of reciprocity. The caxlanes bring their solidarity, and the indigenous open up their community to outsiders. The caxlanes bring material resources and a global outlook on the political scenario; the indigenous share their rich culture and Zapatista way of life. There is a solidarity that swings both ways, but a reciprocity? I'm not sure. We are not one, and we are not the same. There can be sharing and generosity and strong bonds of solidarity built between us, but we also need to recognize the limits of our own capacity to come together. There are insurmountable inequalities, and the caxlanes are the ones who always leave, and the indigenous are the ones who are—and will remain—fucked.

The moon hangs languid over the gentle valley, the fiesta concludes with grand handshakes and eye-to-eye thank yous. We, the volunteers, the water team—the ones who are about to leave for good—chat and sing and potter about the little schoolroom, this fine citadel of nurturing, packing away our fine hopes and desires in preparation for the next project.

Outside we can go to the public tap stand and wash our faces before going to sleep. The simple joy of turning a tap on, the water washing away all worries. The water, the flow, the eternal spring. Zapatista Spring. It's cool and fresh and clear and utterly beautiful. Happiness abounds tonight in this little village.

Maria has been deep in discussion with Don Sisifo outside the schoolroom, and so she is the last to climb into her hammock, blow out the last candle, on this last night.

Is everything OK?

"Yeah no problem. Don Sisifo sums it all up pretty well."

So what did he say?

"He said that despite so many ordeals, he listens to his heart and it allows him to conclude that all is well."

Aftermath.
Solidarity and Its Malcontents

"There are no magic answers, no miraculous methods to overcome the problems we face, just the familiar ones: search for understanding, education, organization, action ... and the kind of commitment that will persist despite the temptations of disillusionment, despite many failures and only limited successes, inspired by the hope of a brighter future." —Noam Chomsky

Deus Ex Machina, *Unwelcome*

An important part of solidarity work, and water projects in particular, is following up on the initial impulse and project. Often this just means being in touch with the Zapatista junta as they act as a conduit for problems related to installed water projects. Equally, if there are particular things the community needs, like new valves or the repair of a broken pump, the requests are relayed through the Zapatista authorities at the local caracol. Sometimes, under special circumstances, water workers will just go straight to the community and check up on the system while paying a social visit.

So it was that we decided to pay Roberto Arenas a visit. Praxedis, Sofia, and I bypass the junta and just hit the road directly for the community. It has been a couple of years since we completed the water system and we have not heard a word from them since. So we just want to go check out the functioning of the system and say hello to Don Sisifo, Doña Dolores, and the whole gang.

Sofia quit her desk job for the NGO in Italy and has come to work for the water projects in Chiapas full time. I have since stopped working on water projects and moved on to a more sedate, though equally challenging activity: parenting.

Things have changed. The new governor of Chiapas, in collaboration with the new president, is exercising a fresh strategy against Zapatismo. The previous, overtly repressive tactics—states of siege, constant military interventions—have been replaced by a more public-relations-oriented version of military occupation. Troops have returned to barracks, and roadblocks are few and far between. But neither has gone away, and other dangers abound for the Zapatistas. State-sponsored paramilitaries are on the rise. These local paramilitaries are usually fellow indigenous campesinos affiliated with pro-government organizations, or sometimes disaffected ex-Zapatistas, but usually they're dispossessed, disgruntled young men attracted to the power of an AK-47. The paramilitaries made their debut on the world stage by killing forty-five indigenous Zapatista supporters (predominantly women and children) in the Acteal massacre of December, 1997.

Since then, belligerent groups of this ilk—armed and trained by pro-government elements—have replaced the military as the primary physical threat for the Zapatista base communities. Where once there were military encampments *outside* the communities, there now are paramilitary groups embedded *within* the communities. Different uniforms, same role—agents of government and state counterinsurgency strategies. The government strategy follows classic textbook counter-insurgency: use paramilitary forces selectively to enforce compliance with the policies or objectives of the government. Tactical employment of low intensity warfare in Chiapas results in shifting the fulcrum of repression from the military to the paramilitaries, one step removed from the State. And crucially, what was first understood as an uprising of indigenous against the Mexican state, is now described in official circles as an "inter-communal conflict." This is the racist narrative promoted by the authorities—*the murderous Indians are killing each other as usual.*

For better or for worse, this means we feel confident enough to drive directly to the community via the jungle canyon road that was so long out of bounds. The migration office outside Ocosingo is now semi-deserted, the barracks outside La Garrucha completely abandoned, and the once-feared military barracks at El Abismo is quiet these days. Even the permanent roadblock outside the base has been removed. So, for the first time ever, we will ride all the way to the community by road and return the same day.

We circumvent these familiar mountains and jungle, but riding to the community inside a car is not nearly the same as hacking one's way there through the undergrowth. Still, nobody is complaining. We sit back and admire the exotic scenery like proper tourists. I ask Sofia how she feels about up and leaving her office in the big city to work here.

"It's fucking great. I'm taking a 500% wage cut [as a full-time water worker she receives a stipend to cover living expenses—not a salary], but loving every minute of it."

"You're also working 500% more than anybody else on the water project," says Praxedis. Oh yeah, these two have hooked up pretty tight, assuming the mantle of the Bonnie and Cyde of the Lacandon Jungle. And Praxedis is correct—Sofia is a stellar addition to the team. My absence, I regret to say, is not felt.

"The fucking NGO industry is a racket. They spend more money on their own salaries and positions than they do the supposed recipients. And half of the projects do more damage than good, like micro-credit schemes getting everyone deeply in debt."

Around midday, we pass the PRI-ista community where we once had disembarked and hiked, somewhat anxiously, over their lands to go the back way to Roberto Arenas. We notice that the remote community is looking a lot more built up, with new concrete houses replacing the traditional wooden or adobe style. One consequence of the Zapatista uprising in this part of the jungle is that the government, in an attempt to win hearts and minds, has thrown lots of funding at non-Zapatista communities in order to entice them away from the influence of the rebels. So the cruel irony is that the standard of living has increased for a lot of indigenous communities around here—providing they are not Zapatista. Much of the government aid comes in the form of bricks and mortar, leading to the increasingly pervasive concretization of the jungle.

Further along the road we arrive at the El Abismo military installations and, sure enough, all is quiet. The great iron gates are shut and the sentry post uninhabited. It feels like some small victory to sail by on our merry way to visit our Zapatista compañeros after all the effort to avoid this place during the project.

The pickup sweeps down the valley. The Jataté is now visible, winding its way further down the basin. We are about a kilometer from Roberto when the trouble begins. We come upon a makeshift roadblock manned by three campesinos who are brandishing semi-automatic rifles and have paliacates tied across their faces.

"Zapatistas, right?" asks Sofia.

"They're not Zapatistas," says Praxedis, ominously. "Zaps don't carry carbines."

We pull up and the first masked man asks where we are going.

Praxedis explains that we are going to a community nearby "to visit friends." He purposefully doesn't reveal whether or not we're going to a Zapatista community.

The gunman is not overtly hostile, just edgy and unfriendly. We are tense, but not really frightened. I mean, we know lots of folks around these parts and we should be able to negotiate our way out of whatever trouble finds us.

"Show me your papers. We have to check your vehicle."

Praxedis passes his fake driver's license and tries to appeal to the gunman's altruistic sentiment.

"We have come a long way to see our friends. We are bringing medicine for their sick child."

Which is kind of true as we have brought some basic medicines just in case anybody in the community needs them.

The other gunman has gone to the rear of the pick-up and is looking inside the back. He returns and talks in his comrade's ear, in Tzeltal.

"What are all the tools and equipment in the back?" asks the first.

"Plumbing tools," replies Praxedis. "We are going to help a friend with his water system."

"In which community?" asks the man, twitching his carbine in the air nonchalantly.

This is the scary moment. If these guys are some kind of nervous Zapatistas, uncertain of who we are, then declaring Roberto Arenas our destination will break the ice, they will know we are compañeros, and everything will be hunky-dory. But if these guys are PRI-istas or paramilitaries then we are fucked, and we will have a lot of negotiating to do. They could detain us or take our stuff. There is not really a threat of violence, or at least there is no precedent of caxlanes being shot up at a makeshift roadblock like this one. Nevertheless, being confronted by men with guns is always nervewracking, but it is even more so now, since it comes as a total surprise.

Another scenario crosses my mind: What if they are just common bandits? Several other solidarity workers have gotten pulled over by bandits and robbed on deserted jungle roads like this one, in the middle of nowhere. Only this isn't nowhere, we're a mere kilometer from Roberto Arenas. Bandits are not known for harming folks, just robbing them blind. We could be left on the side of the road in our underwear, hitching back to Ocosingo. An ignominious thought.

There is not much Praxedis can say. If we are going to get fucked we may as well get fucked for the right reasons.

"Roberto Arenas."

The gunman smiles behind his paliacate and says, "You're not welcome there."

A noise behind us causes us to all look around. The other gunman is removing a heavy sledgehammer and several other tools from the back of our truck.

"We are going to borrow a few tools from you but don't worry, we'll leave them with your friends in Roberto for safe keeping."

"Come on, man," begins Praxedis, opening his door. "Leave the tools..."

Sofia and I are hissing at our compañero to shut the fuck up, close the door, and get us out of here.

The gunman closes the driver-side door and indicates the direction we should go with his carbine.

Thankfully, Praxedis turns off his bravado, and reluctantly turns the pickup around and heads back on the long road to Ocosingo.

"Jesus. What the fuck was that?" I say, flabbergasted and glad to still be in one piece.

"I have no fucking idea. Not bandits, at least not real bandits. Renegade Zapatistas maybe?" says Praxedis.

Sofia looks grim. "The third gunman. The one who didn't come over to the car, I think he looked familiar. I think he was the compa we used to joke resembled a Galician fisherman."

"Fuck it, you're right." I too realize that I vaguely recognized the guy. He stayed away from the car though. He was taller than the other guys, and had the makings of a beard peeking out from the top of his paliacate. But...if it's our old friend, why didn't he present himself and get us out of the jam?

At the crossroads to Ocosingo we turn the other direction to La Garrucha. We need to talk to the Zapatista authorities.

In Garrucha, we bypass the junta and are hurried over to the office of the local Zapatista leader, *el Comandante*.

We sit on the little bench outside the *cuartel*, the EZLN headquarters. We gaze out over the scenic and sweeping valley of La Garrucha and wait our turn to see the jefe. I remember being here many years ago, in a very different era. Originally, in the early days of the insurrection, Garrucha was a Zapatista guerrilla camp. Today

I look out over a quiet, industrious village with a busy medical clinic, a school full of kids, a little library, and a host of other civilian ventures. When I sat here in January of 1995, I would look over a set of wooden huts occupied by a company of young Zapatista guerrillas, all splendidly decked out in their combat uniforms—brown shirts, black pants, black boots, and red paliacates tied around their necks. They all carried their rifles over their shoulders, and contrary to reports, they were not an ill-equipped guerrilla unit—an array of AK-47s and other semi-automatic rifles was visible here for anybody to see. Of course not anybody could stroll into this guerrilla camp. The EZLN were in cease-fire mode and engaged in peace talks with government representatives. The rebels held the bulk of the Lacandon Jungle region and guarded the Zapatista zone with a ring of roadblocks, inside of which there was no government or military presence. For eleven months, from January 1994 to February 1995, it was a de facto Zapatista rebel zone, and I must say, it was very exciting to be here. I was volunteering—yes, you guessed it—on a water project. It was for Garrucha headquarters, and the very first in the region. A straightforward affair, the project was led by a couple of English development workers and went without a hitch.

And I remember sitting outside the same comandante's hut back in January of 1995, heady days in Chiapas indeed. The whiff of the armed uprising was still in the air, and the possibility of revolutionary change abounded. This particular day, the insurgents and militia members were milling around—about a third of them female. There was some great maelstrom going down. It was nothing to do with us; I was merely waiting for the English water woman to finish her business with some EZLN honchos inside. The consternation seemed to center on two young female Zapatista insurgents. They sat beside me on the bench, visibly nervous, one of them crying.

All eyes were focused on her.

Flanked by two bodyguards sporting sparkling AK-47s, the comandante came out, his face concealed by a balaclava. He ordered the women inside, and they shuffled past like two condemned convicts, like dead-women walking...

My English friend filled me in on the scandal: the young *compañera insurgente* had violated an important guerrilla rule. She was pregnant.

What was so bad about that? Wasn't it Subcomandante Marcos himself who joked that the Mexican army could probably overtake the EZLN front lines because all the insurgents would be too busy making love? So you reap what you sow, the compañera is pregnant. Shouldn't everyone be delighted, a child born of such great rebel love?

"I think its more a question of discipline, of military discipline," explained my friend. "And that getting pregnant makes her a useless insurgent, and all the training and time invested in her development as a soldier is wasted. I think that is the problem. Although who knows, it could be something else."

The camp doctor is called over. Later he tells us that he was called upon to do a physical examination and ascertain whether she could still have an abortion. She could not. So the end result is that she is court-martialed and, by way of punishment, stripped of her rank and, I believe, banished back to her community.

It all seemed very harsh to me, and my sympathy was with the poor teen being led away—now without her rifle—weeping on her comrade's shoulder. In disgrace. But then again, they were a guerrilla army back then, premised on hard discipline and obeying commands.

So I sit here on this somewhat historic bench a decade later and face the same masked comandante, although the rifle is gone, as are the armed guards. Now I suppose he is a civilian commander—though he does still seem to exercise a similar sort of authority and command. The junta may be the public face of decision-making, but the decisions often seem to return to this man.

Admittedly, I have only anecdotal evidence to support such a claim. The working of the inner-sanctums of the Zapatistas are, by device, clandestine and secretive, but from what I glean in conversations with other comrades, with friends and colleagues, many important decisions are made by the particular comandante of the region, rather than the relevant community assembly or designated responsables. My own experience living and working alongside the Zapatistas allows me an insight into the mechanisms of power within the community, and I similarly conclude that despite the centrality of the community assembly, people often seem inclined to turn to one particular person, the local EZLN head-honcho, for certain decisions. Old habits—like letting someone else make your decisions for you—die hard, and unfortunately, the practice flies in the face of the much-lauded notion of Zapatista participatory democracy. It is like a system of old-school *caudillismo* (strong man rule) still lingers, like a useless tradition that people cannot quite shake off, despite the democratic aspirations of the movement.

How does one describe a man whose face is hidden by a mask? This man, without a visible nose, mouth, or any other feature, is wholly defined by his eyes. And this comandante has the most intense black eyes that burn into you. His stature is familiar, as it is similar to the other campesinos around him, but this man has a presence that emanates strength and power, and he exudes a kind of natural leader confidence. Rumor portends that at a young age, he emerged as a good orator and catechist in the community church. He must have been bold and daring too, to enter into the EZLN ranks at an early age, and to rise through the ranks. And now he is here, years later, the regional comandante, a position of great local power and prestige. He comes from the community, and he is of the community still—there is no separation or division now that he has a prestigious rank. The mask he wears serves as an equalizing force; he could be any of the campesinos we have met along the way. It is like the mask simultaneously and paradoxically gives him grand authority, but strips him of any individual potency. Hence it stands to reason that the mask the comandante wears should make him more accountable to the community he serves, than is the *caudillo* (local strong man) with a visible face. The power of office lies in the mask, and that mask can be worn by someone else to assume power if the people deem it necessary.

Having finally gained an audience with him, it is clear *el comandante* is not at all amused to hear our tale, and so vents his annoyance. His black eyes burn into us. "You had no permission to go there!"

We were going to check up on the water system, we say in our defense, feeling a little like school kids before the principal.

"We have had some problems with the compañeros there. They are no longer in the organization. They have left. Nobody is working in the region anymore. You had no permission to go there."

Praxedis is not satisfied by this explanation. "That is too bad that they left the organization, but why are they manning armed checkpoints? And why wouldn't they let us enter? They know we are not part of the Zapatista organization, that we are an autonomous project..."

"You are lucky you didn't get shot up, compañeros. We believe they have joined a paramilitary organization."

"Why?" asks Sofia, stunned.

"I don't know. Some compañeros are not committed enough; they sell out, lose faith. We have more than enough compas to take their place."

The comandante has said all he wants on that theme, and changes the subject. He needs to discuss upcoming water projects with Praxedis and Sofia. I am invited to leave, and wait outside.

I sit on the little bench outside the command hut once more. It strikes me that I am spending entirely too much time of my life on this very bockety bench, and it makes me weary. I look out upon this thriving little village, one that is surely a stunning example of autonomy in action and the success of Zapatismo in this region. And yet all I feel is bewildered, deflated, and a little sad. The compañeros of Roberto Arenas, our friends with whom we worked side-by-side, shared toil and celebration, are now the enemy? The implacable Don Sisifo, the valiant Adelita? Paramilitaries? It seems all wrong.

I light up a last cigarette and muse on life's little ironies. I can only speculate as to why they left the Zapatistas and switched sides, but one thing strikes me as cynically amusing: we worked our arses off for three whole months building up the infrastructure of an anti-Zapatista community. This is, from a philosophical point of view, absurd.

Too Long A Sacrifice

Some 300,000 hectares of land was taken over by the EZLN and their fellow travelers during their uprising in 1994. This "recuperated" land, as the Zapatistas refer to it, was carefully re-distributed to landless peasants and communities over the next few years in an organized, systematic manner by the EZLN. But the Zapatista uprising was not just a land-grab—as righteous as that is in its own right, considering the near feudal conditions in the region—but was also about freedom. Winning the land was the easy part, achieving freedom was the bigger task. Little by lit-tle they built up autonomous structures of governance that, over time, began to look like the kind of freedom they had in mind. "Land and Freedom," the cry of the original Mexican revolution, had begun to take form in this small state at the end of Mexico, this nowhere place off the map—and it represented a problem for the authorities. It wasn't the small amount of land involved, but the threat that their good example would spread throughout the country.

The counter-insurgency strategy, employed by the gov-ernment and its repressive forces, focused on reclaiming that liberated land and enclosing the autonomous initiative at its source, and crushing any autonomous rhizomes that appeared elsewhere.

What happened in Roberto Arenas can, on one level, be understood within the auspices of that struggle between Zapa-tista emancipation and state counter-insurgency. If the Zapa-tistas were building their model of emancipation and autonomy on the basis of communally held lands (*ejido*), the government undermined that effort by attempting to privatize community land tenure.

Since Aztec times, the ejido system has been a common Mex-ican practice, protected by Article 27 of the Mexican Constitu-tion, which was introduced after the Mexican revolution of 1910. Communally owned land could not be alienated (sold, or taken by a bank for default on a loan), thereby protecting the fabric of the community from land speculation. Article 27 was changed in preparation for the implementation of the neo-liberal North American Free Trade Agreement (NAFTA) in 1994, so that ejido land could be privatized. The Zapatistas resisted this attempt to break up traditional communities, particularly indigenous communities, refusing to enter into the government-initiated programs for privatizing ejido land titles.

The government offers seductive incentives through the *Agraria Reforma*, handing out privatized land titles like candy.[1] For many impoverished campesinos the offer becomes too enticing—like money for nothing—and so they succumb to the scheme. The Zapatistas threaten any communities who enter into the privatization scheme with expulsion from the organization, and the result, as hoped for by the counter-insurgency plans, is a hemorrhaging of the rebel ranks.

When representatives of Roberto Arenas went to the Agraria Reforma to title their land—part of the land recuperated in 1994—they not only renounced their affiliation with the Zapatistas, but were also forced into a vulnerable position. More sinister elements enter, the ex-Zapatistas are offered protection and arms. Protection, in this case, from the Organization for the Defense of Indigenous and Campesino Rights (OPDDIC, its Spanish acronym), a paramilitary organization set up by pro-government elements for the purpose of protecting the privatized territory.

Once the land is privatized, the way is opened up for capital investment and neo-liberal development. The Lacandon Rainforest is enormously biodiverse, and is an important "lung" for carbon exchange in North America. Capital is interested in exploiting the region for a host of reasons, from developing tourism to industrial farming, mineral extraction, and bio-prospecting. The bountiful supply of sweet water has attracted the attention of transnational bottling companies like Coca-Cola. Sitting on such valuable real estate, villages like Roberto Arenas are targeted by bigger players in this macro-conflict.

While the big picture conflict is daunting, the pressure on the indigenous community also comes from within. More light is shed on the micro-story some time later, on yet another visit to the region. This time, we are attending a Zapatista encuentro, a gathering in the La Garrucha caracol to celebrate the fourteenth anniversary of the January 1st, 1994 uprising, and this one focuses on women within the movement. A few thousand people take part in this annual rebel gathering, which serves to demonstrate the Zapatistas continued support, and is a harbinger for their political direction—a kind of collective "State of the Union Address," but in the jungle,

---

1. We must presume that the community went to the Agraria Reforma, as this is the standard procedure to follow when entering into a process of titling community-held lands.

and overseen by a multitude of masked indigenous compañeros. And it is always nice to see lots of folks from the communities and the caxlanes who return for this inveterate social occasion.

Indeed, on this occasion, we are delighted to reacquaint with some of the water project volunteers who have returned to visit. Tlaxlocaztla tells us she has completed her studies and now works in academia in Mexico City. She is engaged to marry some highly regarded Marxist professor from the most prestigious university. So even if she didn't find her place amongst the indigenous peasantry of Chiapas, at least she seems to have fallen in well with the radical bourgeois intelligentsia of the capital city.

"Is Nebula here with you?" I ask, probably a little too eagerly. (Oh yeah, I should add here that when the water project in Roberto finished, she and I went on the town for a few days and nights. There was late night debauchery as we trawled San Cristobal's seedier nocturnal establishments, and plenty of posh was consumed. I've missed her.)

"No, man. Haven't you heard? She is holed up in Gaza. She is the shit, man. Awesome."

Omar is also here, and he is now a very active member in his local Zapatista support group. He has returned to Chiapas several times, often accompanying football team delegations who tour the autonomous region playing local squads. He has swapped his camera for a soccer ball and tells us it's a lot more fun to play footy with the compas than film them.

"Maybe Josef did me a favor!" he laughs.

Speaking of whom, any word on the inimitable Josef? No, not a word; nobody has heard anything. He has disappeared without a trace.

"Maybe he joined OPDDIC with Don Sisifo and the crew?" jokes Praxedis.

"What?!"

Oh yeah, we have yet to inform them of the bad news about Roberto Arenas.

"Damn!" says Tlaxlocaztla. "If I could have written that turnabout into my thesis, it would have been killer!"

Omar is a little more considerate. "That is really depressing. Who would ever have thought such a thing? Things must be very hard for the community."

I keep a hopeful eye for any of the compañeros from Roberto Arenas. Often affiliation shifts within communities and so maybe the compas have returned to the Zapatista fold. But alas, no sign of familiar faces. I am saddened, not least because compañeras like Adelita would have really appreciated this gathering, which is led by indigenous women and focuses on their struggle. Praxedis and I go over to the EZLN cuartel and request permission to visit or talk to someone from the community of Roberto Arenas, but are refused. The EZLN compañeros confirm that they are still part of the enemy OPDDIC organization. And some things never change—we sit on that bockety bench—but others do: the comandante is gone. Nobody will say what has happened to him, but he is no longer the jefe. The people decided it was time to remove him, is all we can glean from one compa.

So nobody from Roberto Arenas is to be found, or indeed that region, except—and you are going to love this, dear reader—our old friend the organ grinder, the synthesizer man from the party is here at the encuentro! I didn't recognize him, but Sofia and Praxedis point him out, "Look! It's Elvis!" He is not wearing his party suit and thankfully is bereft of his synthesizer.

We greet him as if we were long lost friends, and after a while, I feel bad about maligning him so because he is such a lovely man, chatty and generous. We finally ascertain his relationship to Roberto Arenas: although he hails from a different region, he is Doña Dolores's cousin. We ply him with questions as to what has happened and why.

"I only know a little, from what I have heard from my cousin, but I will share it with you…"

In the background, a female singer is serenading us with beautiful renditions of Violeta Para's "Gracias a la Vida." The sound system is perfect, the live musicians terrific, and not a synthesizer in sight anywhere. Zapatista fiestas are on the up!

"I think that the compañeros in Roberto Arenas felt they were just giving and giving all the time to the organization—the Zapatista organization—and not getting much back in return. They had received the land at the beginning, and they were content with that, but then the organization made many demands of them. They were already dissatisfied before they were presented the water system. I think the water was an attempt by the leadership to keep them in the organization."

It is true that Zapatista affiliation does require a level of commitment and sacrifice that is difficult to maintain over the long years of resistance. The base communities provide food and equipment for the EZLN, and members of the community must participate in various committees, initiatives, and mobilizations convened by the organization. Even the travel expenses to attend these meetings, accrued over time, are often too much for the impoverished peasant base to afford. Furthermore, ideological affiliation to the Zapatistas means refusing any government or state services and handouts. As the government floods neighboring non-Zapatista communities and villages with alms, in the form of concrete and laminated roofing—think: hearts and minds—the non-recipient Zapatista communities take the brunt of organizational affiliation even more, their sacrifice more obvious.

We are silent for a moment, dwelling on the man's words. I recall the poet Yeats's criticism of Irish revolutionaries: "too long a sacrifice can make a stone of the heart."

"They seemed such diehard Zapatistas," says Sofia, "so proud of their achievements and participation in the insurrection."

"And they will tell you still they are diehard Zapatistas. But they have had enough of some comandante or jefe always telling them what they should or must do. There comes a point when they say 'no more.' Always asking them to give their time and take orders and they asked what were they getting in return?"

"Land and Freedom?" I suggest.

"Doña Dolores told me that she is still 100% Zapatista, but that the government was prepared to deliver more to the community than the Zapatistas. The government promised electricity and materials to build houses. They are constructing a hammock bridge over the river."

"The price of betrayal: a hammock bridge," muses Praxedis.

Elvis has told us as much as he can. We ask him to convey our good wishes to Doña Dolores, and our hope that she and her community come back. He promises to pass on the message.

One last question: "Is the water system working well?"

"Perfect. You did a great job."

Scant conciliation.

"Are you performing tonight, Don Elvis?"

"No, not tonight. They didn't invite me," he says, a bit forlorn. And we all breathe a sigh of relief. Proving an earlier assertion of mine wrong, the fiesta this night in the caracol is a blast, and people dance all night—we all do. It feels like a whole new era of post-synthesizer party glasnost.

End Words:
The Journey Itself is Enough?

Success stories are hard to come by in the much-disputed field of international solidarity, but here, in this one small narrative of the project in Roberto Arenas I thought we had one. A story worth telling. A story worth remembering.

We were told to go somewhere by the Zapatista authorities and we did it, in good faith. And something we don't understand happened in that little rebel village. There was an unexpected change in the narrative; things fall apart and suddenly nothing makes sense anymore.

We are thrown into confusion. We are left doubting our agency, questioning everything. Solidarity is unity of purpose or togetherness, and as we worked together in Roberto Arenas, we, the caxlanes, thought we were building Zapatista autonomy, and the community thought we were building...well, a water system. Two ways of looking at the same thing. It feels like falling victim to some overarching prank, an elaborate conceit whereupon we were led to believe all along that we were working to strengthen Zapatismo, while some devious hand was instead overseeing some convoluted plot to undermine the project. Our solidarity accomplishment morphed into a solidarity conceit.

So what are we going to do then? Return to Roberto Arenas in the dark of night and sabotage the water system? Of course not. I think of the children, of Marisol and Jorge, or the elderly people, the sick Doña Consuela, the health responsable Don Job and his proud assertion of having nurtured "ten Zapatista children." There is no doubt whatsoever that these people deserve basic necessities, like a supply of fresh unpolluted water, like anybody in the world, beyond political affiliation, beyond politics. It is a basic human right. So what we were doing was not political solidarity, as we imagined, but simply providing a basic service, that was lacking, for poor people. Ironically, at the end of the project, when Don Sisifo thanked us for helping them, the poor of Chiapas, by presenting them with a community water system, he was fully correct.

I find myself returning again to that millennia-old mythological figure in order to shed light on our current conundrum. Previously, I evoked Camus's interpretation of Sisyphus as an absurd hero, a "proletarian of the Gods, powerless and rebellious"[2] and found in Don Sisifo, and his ilk who form the Zapatista base, one embodiment of the myth. And now, considering the recent turn of events, does the metaphor still apply? Can Don Sisifo as non-Zapatista "counter-revolutionary" still be thought of as an embodiment of the Sisyphus myth? Or, to put it another way: can a "traitor" to the Zapatista cause still be considered a metaphorical "proletarian of the gods," etc.?

And I think yes, even as an ex-Zapatista, the image persists. Even as a peasant who rebels against the Zapatistas. Don Sisifo, like all those disaffected rebels who come before and after him, embodies Sisyphus's endless struggle, powerlessness and rebellious scorn for his fate and the Gods who condemned him to a life of toil.

From this perspective it is possible to reflect on Don Sisifo and his community's defection from Zapatista ranks beyond the most knee-jerk reaction, beyond labelling him a counterrevolutionary, a traitor, a Judas betrayer. Of course it is more complicated than that. Just as becoming a Zapatista is an act of rebellion, so too is leaving the Zapatistas behind. These peasants are still as they were to begin with—marginalized, impoverished, and despised. A long time ago, the Zapatistas offered them hope, and so they joined. And when the protracted Zapatista struggle stopped offering hope and instead demanded more sacrifice and less benefit, they turned elsewhere in an attempt to improve their lot. Don Sisifo and the community of Roberto Arenas continue their endless struggle. Of course I am sad and disappointed that they left the Zapatista

2. Camus, Albert. *The Myth of Sisyphus.*

organization, but I don't condemn them for their desertion. They have left the Zapatistas, but not the struggle—their struggle as indigenous peasants who are fighting for a better life. Maybe it was the Zapatistas who let down this Sisyphus, and not he the Zapatistas.

I'm not trying to negate the great Zapatista project. There have been many brilliant experiences working in solidarity with the Zapatistas. Usually one hears rose-tinted accounts from ardent propagandists, and this one is just another story but from a different angle, or with a different ending. I choose to focus on this particular story because I think it is—in its complexity—an instructive story. I'm still a Zapatista supporter, and an advocate for solidarity with the organization, albeit conditional solidarity. I remember the experience of those who worked in solidarity with the FSLN in Nicaragua in the 1980s, people who are now embarrassed to be associated with what the FSLN has become twenty years later. Political organizations change, and sometimes not in ways that radicals would like them to. Better to remain in conditional solidarity with the organization, however attractive their

professed political platform may be, while at the same t
careful to avoid romanticising peasant or indigenous str
we remember that the process of international solidarit
revolution, a question and not an answer, then it too can realize its
capacity to be an exploration in the creation of dignity—as theorist
John Holloway has written.

Despite political failure, was the project in Roberto Arenas
worthwhile? Yes! What is three months labor and some $6,000 in
the greater scheme of things? For this one water project that fails
politically, a dozen more that we have overseen remain in Zapatista
hands. One learns a little bit of humility and the need to resist disillusionment, to remain committed and sustain hope.

I imagine Sisyphus pushing the rock up the mountain for eternity, but this time not with our resilient protagonist Don Sisifo in
mind. Here is a man who struggles endlessly with the same labor,
knowing it will all come to nothing, and yet, as Camus said, refutes
this futile task by scorning the gods that condemned him to it,
finding satisfaction in the job itself. Camus exhorts us to imagine
Sisyphus teaching a "higher fidelity that negates the gods and raises
rocks," and thus, he is content. His endless struggle is an act of rebellion against despair. To rebel is enough, and Camus's Sisyphus
understands, "the struggle itself toward the heights is enough to
fill a mans heart."

Must it be so for revolutionary solidarity? No doubt we are
content in our work of resistance, even if we don't always get results and the shadow of futility looms. Just as we rebels are drawn
to Chiapas and the Zapatistas for the allure of revolutionary promise and changing the world anew, we engage in the process of pushing big rocks up mighty mountains and no doubt the passion of the
struggle fills our hearts. But is to rebel enough?

No, it is not enough, never enough. Fuck Sisyphus. As rebels,
we resist, but as revolutionaries, our task is to change history, in-
vent new myths, and not be condemned to repeat history time and
again.

One more big push, compañeros and compañeras—to rupture
the paradigm, to propel that rock over the cusp, down the other
side of the mountain and towards pastures new.

Ramor Ryan is an Irish writer and translator based in Chiapas, Mexico. His book *Clandestines: The Pirate Journals of an Irish Exile* was published by AK Press in 2006. Contact him at ramorx@hotmail.com.

Support AK Press!

AK Press is one of the world's largest and most productive  anarchist publishing houses. We're entirely worker-run and demo-cratically managed. We operate without a corporate structure—no boss, no managers, no bullshit. We publish close to twenty books every year, and distribute thousands of other titles published by other like-minded independent presses from around the globe.

The Friends of AK program is a way that you can directly contribute to the continued existence of AK Press, and ensure that we're able to keep publishing great books just like this one! Friends pay a minimum of $25 per month, for a minimum three month period, into our publishing account. In return, Friends automatically receive (for the duration of their membership), as they appear, one free copy of every new AK Press title. They're also entitled to a 20% discount on everything featured in the AK Press Distribution catalog and on the web-site, on any and every order. You or your organization can even sponsor an entire book if you should so choose!

There's great stuff in the works—so sign up now to become a Friend of AK Press, and let the presses roll!

Won't you be our friend? Email friendsofak@akpress.org for more info, or visit the Friends of AK Press website: http://www.akpress.org/programs/friendsofak

CLANDESTINES: THE PIRATE JOURNALS OF AN IRISH EXILE

2006 | AK Press | ISBN: 9781904859550 | $15.95 | 280 pgs

"Fleeing Berlin on the late night train to Paris—and me a fugitive with a fake ticket—is perhaps, I reflect, the most appropriate way to leave the subterranean life in Berlin and renew once more as I would, in Chiapas, Mexico. If clandestinity is about moving furtively in the shadows while keeping one step ahead of the forces of repression, law, and order, then in Berlin I learned how it is a fleeting tactic to strike like lightning and retreat safely—the surreptitious exit from the control zone. As a long-term strategy, clandestinity is about protecting ourselves, our rebel spaces and allowing the seed to germinate underground. This is a lesson learned with powerful consequences in Chiapas."—*from the book*

As much an adventure story as an unofficial chronicle of modern global resistance movements, Clandestines spirits the reader into subterranean locales, carefully weaving the narrative through illicit encounters and public bacchanals. From the teeming squats of Berlin, to intrigue in the Zapatista Autonomous Zone, a Croatian Rainbow Gathering on the heels of the G8 protests in Genoa, mutiny on the high seas, the Quixotic ambitions of a Kurdish guerilla camp, the contradictions of Cuba, and the neo-liberal nightmare of post-war(s) Central America we see everywhere a world in flux, struggling to be reborn.

"At once celebratory and self-critical, *Clandestines* offers a geography lesson of the shadows, where borders are disregarded, revolution is in the air, and adventure is always just around the corner."—Jennifer Whitney, co-author of *We Are Everywhere: The Irresistible Rise of Global Anticapitalism*

"I'm convinced that all we need is about a hundred more Ramors and the revolution would commence tomorrow."—David Graeber, *Fragments of an Anarchist Anthropology*